BIGFOOT:
West Coast Wild Men

A History of Wild Men, Gorillas,
and Other Hairy Monsters in
California, Oregon, and Washington State.

Compiled, written, and illustrated by
Timothy Renner

CreateSpace Independent Publishing Platform

ISBN: 1983434094
ISBN-13: 978-1983434099

DEDICATION

To James K. and James R.
who follow strange footprints into strange places with me ...
And to Seriah Azkath and Joshua Cutchin who always offer help, advice,
and an alternate view of the strange and mysterious.

CONTENTS

ACKNOWLEDGMENTS

Edited by Catherine Diehl.

Guest commentary on the first article in chapter 6 by Joshua Cutchin.

Cover design by Brian Magar.

A NOTE ON SPELLING AND GRAMMAR - AND A DISCLAIMER

Regarding "bigfoot" - since this is the name of a group of animals, not one individual, I do not capitalize bigfoot. I also use "bigfoot" as both the singular and plural (like "deer"). Some other authors have tried to standardize the grammar for bigfoot, insisting the plural is variously "bigfeet" or "bigfoots", however to my ears both of these terms hold more problems than simply using the term bigfoot universally as the singular and plural. Until the Oxford English Dictionary weighs in on the subject, I will stand on "bigfoot". Pun intended.

Since the bulk of this volume is taken from old newspaper articles, in most cases I have kept much of the grammar and spelling as they appeared in the original articles. I believe this retains the flavor of the originals - as does the columned layout. There is something special about reading these old articles. It is very much a window to the past, and I wanted to keep as much of that old view in the window as possible.

Along with the grammar and spelling of the past come the biases and outdated attitudes of long ago. I am, unfortunately for my straining book and record shelves, a bit of a completist. I have made, to the best of my abilities, a complete survey of early "wild-man" articles concerning Pennsylvania. Amongst these reprinted articles you will find some words and attitudes that we no longer consider politically correct - veering, at times, into outright racism. I have included these articles only for their references to what I believe are bigfoot creatures. Reading them today can be an eye-opening experience both in how far we have come as a society and in how many of these hurtful stereotypes have survived amongst modern racists. In no way should the inclusion of said articles be taken as an endorsement or tacit acceptance of the racism, xenophobia, and other backwards beliefs displayed therein. My interest, and hopefully the interest of the reader as well, lies with tales of mysterious creatures, not with the biases and attitudes of racist humans.

INTRODUCTION

Seeing as this is my second book in as many years featuring historical bigfoot articles, faithful readers and collectors of bigfoot literature may notice some similar words, phrases, and themes repeated both in the articles themselves and in my own commentary. I cannot assume anyone has read the first book or - if this is being read some years from now - any of the other books I intend to write on the subject.

As regards the articles, I believe this repetition speaks to a consistency of the reports. Sometimes this is due to the scant information provided in the articles - often the reporters just do not relay all of the information we would like to read - but other times these articles report behaviors of the creature which are seen elsewhere - in other bigfoot reports from the past and in stories from modern witnesses. These are the instances which become most exciting for me as a researcher and enthusiast of all things bigfoot. These are dots being connected through time and showing a picture of consistent patterns of behavior on the part of bigfoot creatures.

It is these witness reports - new and old - which may be our most valuable resource of bigfoot evidence. Footprint casts, hair samples, and scat are all well and good, but they only really tell us, at best, some anatomical or dietary information; and more often, simply that *something* was in a specific area. Perhaps someday we will get a confirmed DNA sample or photographic evidence deemed legitimate by mainstream science, but I am not holding my breath. Until such time, we have the words of witnesses. Many of these witnesses seem to be reporting things which not only look the same (large, hair covered, humanoid) but express the same kinds of behaviors. Year after year after year.

The previous book - and what has become the first in a series of like volumes - is titled "Bigfoot in Pennsylvania". I spent some wordage in my introduction to that volume declaring my ignorance as to just what bigfoot *are*. Undiscovered North American ape? Jungian archetype? Dimension-hopping hairy thing? Relict hominid? Something else entirely? I confess, I have come no further in my willingness to commit to one camp or another. The truth is, I do not know what bigfoot are - and neither does anyone else, no matter how loudly they may proclaim otherwise.

Stories of hunters shooting bigfoot creatures always end with the body disappearing - either confiscated by mysterious and ominous government organizations or, presumably, retrieved by other creatures. Bigfoot DNA samples are often lost by labs. When not lost, the results always seem to be returned as contaminated or otherwise shown to be a bear, human, or other natural animal. No photographic evidence has proved conclusive and given the increasingly advanced technology available to consumers, computer generated and/or augmented imagery may mean no film or photograph of bigfoot will ever be accepted as evidence to mainstream science.

There are many, many people dedicated to researching the topic who will argue that DNA studies *have* been done - or that, for instance, the Patterson-Gimlin film *has* been proven to show something that couldn't be a human in a costume. I understand. It's not me you have to convince folks; it's the mainstream. Mainstream science doesn't like weirdness though and, like it or not, bigfoot comes hand in hand with a lot of weirdness. From the disappearing bodies and DNA mentioned above to reports of UFOs, orbs, and other mystery lights in conjunction with the creatures to the apparent fact that bigfoot creatures can somehow detect and avoid trail cams … the list goes on and on. As I said, I do not know what bigfoot is, but I do know bigfoot is surrounded by weird phenomena, strange coincidences, and far more questions than answers.

All of that said, whatever it is, I believe it is real. Large, hair-covered creatures have been reported by men for as long as we have been keeping records. We just didn't always call them by the same name. Most readers will be familiar with the terms bigfoot and Sasquatch - used interchangeably since the latter half of the 20th century in Canada and the U.S. - and the Yeti or abominable snowman from Asia. Bigfoot enthusiasts know of the Yowie from Australia, the Almasty from central Asia, and probably various First Nations names for bigfoot or bigfoot-like creatures (Windigo, Stone Giants, etc.)

In the 1800s, in America, most people wouldn't have been familiar with First Nations legends, much less their names for bigfoot creatures. They wouldn't have used the terms "bigfoot" or "Sasquatch". When they saw something hairy and upright-walking with manlike features and hands, what would they call it? Sometimes they called them monsters or hairy giants but most often they called them "wild men". There seemed to be a general idea that if a human left society to live in the wilderness he or she would soon grow hair upon their body like an animal, lose the power of speech, and turn as wild as the other creatures of the forest.

Here we get reports of naked "madmen" running through the forests, screaming, and stealing livestock. Sometimes these wild men are reported clothed in animal skins or tattered rags - I believe this could be body hair misidentified as torn clothing or perhaps prudish Victorian and Edwardian era newspapermen adding clothes to their wild people so as not to cause scandal or offend their readers.

In the late 1800s as reports of the mountain gorilla begin to reach America - and as people begin to see gorillas in photographs, zoos, or traveling menageries - there begins a subtle shift. Suddenly people have a name to put to these creatures. Some of the "wild-man" reports become "gorilla" reports. Interestingly, there is another shift in the wake of the popularity of Hollywood horror movies in the 1940s and 1950s and the creatures are often reported as "monsters" until the 1970s when "bigfoot" and "Sasquatch" enter the popular vocabulary.

However, the most common term found in the reports in this volume, is the "wild man". This presents a problem for me, as the compiler, and you, as a reader. Sometimes "wild man" really did refer to a human, sane or otherwise, judged by his appearance or actions to be "wild". Sometimes a "wild man" was simply a mountain man who had grown his hair long and wore a beard. Sometimes these wild people really were escaped from a mental hospital or other institution. I did not, by any stretch, simply include every mention of a "wild man" I could find in old newspapers. For every report of a "wild man" which could have been a bigfoot, I discarded probably 20 reports which undoubtedly described a human. That said, I am certain that not every "wild man" report herein refers to a bigfoot creature. Some of these reports could refer to feral humans, escaped patients or other people just living outside the bounds of normal society. I have added commentary in places noting why I think the reports may refer to a bigfoot creature; however, I leave it to the reader to make up his own mind.

No matter your conclusions, I hope that the casual reader and devoted bigfoot enthusiast alike finds as much to like in these old articles as I. Strange tales, hairy monsters, and wild men abound in the pages following - words from the past preserved like footprint casts for us to analyze all these years later.

I. IT WAS IN THE IMAGE OF A MAN, BUT IT COULD NOT HAVE BEEN HUMAN

CALIFORNIA 1866 - 1879

☞ There is a wild man living in Toulumne County.   He has a secluded spot to hide in, and lives on whatever he can find.[1]

————◆————

WILDMAN   — We learn from good authority that a wild man has been seen at Crow Canyon, near Mount Diablo. Several attempts have been made to capture him, but as yet have proved unsuccessful.   His tracks measure thirteen inches.[2]

————◆————

An item appeared in the San Joaquin *Republican* the other day stating that a wild man had been seen in some part of San Joaquin County, and we afterward noticed the statement copied into several other papers, with brief comments indicating disbelief in the report.

We must confess to a want of credulity on our own part also as to the exact correctness of the item at the time, but we were yesterday placed in possession of certain information which leads us to believe that there may be some foundation for the report. As our columns are somewhat crowded this morning, we will give the reports as we received them and as briefly as possible.

F.J. Hildreth and Samuel De Groot, of Washington Corners, in this county, while out hunting on Orias Timbers Creek in Stanislaus County about three weeks ago, discovered footprints along the bank of the creek resembling the impressions of a human being's feet. Mr. Hildreth, who gave us this information, states that the tracks were like those of a human being with the exception that the impressions of the toes were much larger.

Hildreth afterward became separated from his companion, and upon proceeding some distance up the creek, saw a few yards ahead of him what he believed to be gorillas. If the description Mr. Hildreth has given us of these animals is true, he is certainly warranted in believing them to be that species of animal. Mr. De Groot also reports that he saw the same objects and is positive that they are gorillas. The appearance of these strange animals in that neighborhood is notorious and that they are gorillas is firmly believed by a great many people in the vicinity.

A number of old hunters have started out to capture them, and we are promised whatever further facts may occur as soon as the party returns. The above we gathered from various parties, and whether true or not, there are many persons in the neighborhood of the Washington Corners who firmly believe that the animals referred to are veritable gorillas.[3]

————————◆————————

CALIFORNIA GORILLAS

"An Old Hunter," who vouches for the truth of the story, writes to the *Antioch Ledger*, averring that the statement about a gorilla having been seen among the mountains at the head of Orestrinba Creek, and in Crow Canyon, is strictly true. He says:

I positively assure you that this gorilla, or wild man, or whatever you choose to call it, is no myth. I know that it exists, and that there are at least two of them, having seen them both at once, not a year ago. Their existence has been reported at times for the past twenty years, and I have heard it said that, in early days, an ourang-outang escaped from a ship on the southern coast; but the creature I have seen is not that animal, and if it was, where did he get his mate? — import her as web-foots do their wives? Last fall I was hunting in the mountains about twenty miles south of here, and camped five or six days in one place, as I have done every season for the past fifteen years. Several times I returned to my camp, after a hunt, and saw that the ashes and charred sticks from the fire-place had been scattered about. An old hunter notices such things, and very soon gets curious to know the cause. Although my bedding and traps and little stores were not disturbed, that I could see, I was anxious to learn what or who it was that so regularly visited my camp, for clearly the half-burned sticks and cinders could not scatter themselves about. I saw no tracks near camp, as the hard ground covered with dry leaves would show none. So I started on a circle round the place, and three hundred yards off, deep in sand, I struck the tracks of a man's feet, as I supposed — bare, and of immense size. Now I was curious, sure, and resolved to lay for this barefooted visitor. I accordingly took position on a hillside, some sixty or seventy yards from the fire, and hid in the brush, I waited and watched. Two hours or more I sat there, and wondered if the owner of the bare feet would come again, and whether he imagined what an interest he had created in my inquiring mind, and, finally, what possessed him to be prowling about there with no shoes on. The fire-place was on my right, and the spot where I saw the tracks was on my left, hid by bushes. It was in this direction that my visitor would appear there, and besides, it was easier to sit and face that way. Suddenly I was startled by a shrill whistle, such as boys produce with two fingers under their tongues, and turning quickly, I ejaculated, "Good God!" as I saw the object of my solicitude standing beside my fire, erect, and looking suspiciously around. It was in the image of a man, but it could not have been human. I was never so benumbed with astonishment before. The creature, whatever it was, stood fully five feet high, and disproportionately broad and square at the shoulders, with arms of great length. The legs were very short and the body long. The head was small compared to the rest of the creature, and appeared to be set upon his shoulders without a neck. The whole was covered in dark brown and cinnamon colored hair, quite long on some parts, that on the head standing in a shock and growing down close to the eyes, like a Digger Indian's. As I looked he threw his head back and whistled again, and then stooped and grasped a stick from the fire. This he swung round and round, until the fire on the end had gone out, when he repeated the maneuver. I was dumb, almost, and could only look. Fifteen minutes I sat and watched him, as he whistled and scattered my fire about. I could easily have put a bullet through his head, but why should I kill him? Having amused himself, apparently, all he desired, with my fire, he started to go and having gone a short distance, he returned and was joined by another — a female, unmistakably — when they both turned and walked past me, within twenty yards of where I sat, and disappeared in the brush. I could not have had a better opportunity to observe them, as they were unconscious of my presence. Their only object in visiting my camp seemed to be to amuse themselves with swinging lighted sticks around. I have told this story many times since then, and it has often raised an incredulous smile; but I have met one person who has seen the mysterious creatures, and a dozen who have come across their tracks at various places between here and Pacheco Pass.[4]

———————◆———————

A GORILLA

Was seen in the Cedar Mountain range about twenty miles south of here, a few nights since. It was about 2 o'clock in the morning, the moon shining very brightly. The two men had camped out in the mountains and had a large fire burning, when the gorilla came close to them — so near that they could see it very distinctly. It stood looking at them for a few moments, and then ran away, upright, like a man.[5]

———————◆———————

Napa has a wild woman, who goes about the country au naturel.[6]

———————◆———————

THE WILD MAN OF THE SIERRAS

———

He is Seen in the Eastern Part of Tulare County by a Reliable Citizen

The wild man who has been seen so often in the mountains east of here for the last few years, and who has incorrectly been stated to be a species of gorilla, was seen again recently by William Downing near Squaw Valley. He was engaged in picking thimbleberries and was perfectly naked. He was covered all over with long black hair and had long gray whiskers. He is a white man.

He is large and powerful

and at least six feet high. His finger nails have grown out several inches in length. Mr. Downing was within twenty feet of him when he raised up from picking berries. He stood perfectly still and looked at Mr. Downing some time and then turned and started to run. Mr. Downing was sitting down picking berries at the time himself, when the wild creature raised up out of below the bushes near him. He had not seen him before. Mr. Downing was out hunting and was well armed. He is a gentleman of undoubted veracity. Many others of our citizens have at different times caught sight of this monster. William Arnold, an old and well-known citizen, saw him some time ago sitting on top of a large rock engaged in the highly romantic and to him no doubt delightful occupation of scratching himself.

He is a constant terror to the Indians in the mountains eastward, who all have either seen or know of his existence. They tell the most marvelous stories of his performances. They think he is either the devil or some dead white man whose ghost has returned to annoy them. There can be no doubt of the reality of this wonderful wild man as he has been seen so often by the most credible witnesses. A short time ago John G. Knox,

our efficient Deputy County Clerk, while driving rapidly in a buggy above Ash Springs Hill overtook a man running as though frightened almost to death. On inquiry the man told him he had just encountered a terrible wild man or the Devil, and that it was enough to frighten anybody. Mr. Knox took the man into his buggy, and on telling the story at the next house the gentleman there said he himself had seen the same creature. Many persons residing in that region have seen him at various times. We suggest that an effort be made to capture him. His range is pretty well known and his capture could, no doubt, be effected without a very great effort.[7]

———————◆———————

The "wild man," of which so many accounts have been published, has at last been captured, as Mr. Charles Converse informs us. It turns out to be a species of nondescript very like a bear, although it entirely lacks arms or fore legs, and walks upright like a man. Mr. Converse thinks it is a deformed bear. Messrs. Shaft (or Shaffe) and Johnson, who captured him will be in town today. They propose to sell their "catch" to Woodward, and will telegraph to that gentleman in regard to the lusus naturae they have secured. They had to shoot and wound him before catching him. Mr. Converse came down from the mountains on horseback and passed the captors of the "What is it" on the way down with a team. When they arrive we should be able to learn the full particulars in regard to this new wonder of the Sierras.[8]

———————◆———————

THE MISSING LINK

———

Interview of a California Hunter with a Gorilla-Like Wild Man

———

A correspondent of the San Diego *Union* writes as follows concerning a "wild man" recently seen in the mountains in that county. "About ten days ago Turner Helm and myself were in the mountains about ten miles east of Warner's ranch on a prospecting tour, looking for the extension of a quartz lode which had been found by parties some time before. When we were separated, about a half a mile apart — the wind blowing very hard at the time — Mr. Helm, who was walking along looking down at the ground, suddenly

HEARD SOMEBODY WHISTLE.

Looking up he saw 'something' sitting on a large boulder about fifteen or twenty paces from him. He supposed it to be some kind of animal and immediately came down on him with his needle gun. The object immediately rose to its feet and proved to be a man. This man appeared to be covered all over with coarse black hair, seemingly two or three inches long and thick; he was a man of medium size, and rather fine features — not at all like those of an Indian, but more like an American or Spaniard. They stood gazing at each other for a few moments when Mr. Helm spoke to

THE SINGULAR CREATURE

first in English, and then in Spanish, and then in Indian, but the man remained silent. He then advanced toward Mr. Helm, who not knowing what his intentions might be, again came down on him with the gun to keep him at a distance. The man stopped as though he knew there was danger. Mr. Helm called to me, when

THE WILD MAN

went over the hill and was soon out of sight and made good his escape. We had frequently before

7

seen this man's tracks in that part of the mountains, but had supposed them to be tracks of an Indian. Mr. Helm is a man of unquestioned veracity.[9]

————————◆————————

A WILD MAN

————

On Saturday we met a gentleman who lives on the west side of San Joaquin, about seven miles west of Hill's Ferry, who made the following statement: While in the Coast Range, about ten days ago, hunting, he and his companion encamped on the side of a ravine near the summit of the range. In the morning they discovered smoke lower down the ravine, and, upon going out upon the side of the hill to ascertain the origin of it, they discovered an object which puzzled them to name, and as their curiosity became excited they crept carefully toward it, in order to satisfy themselves what kind of animal they had discovered. By creeping upon the ground they were able to approach within one hundred yards, when, to their astonishment, they found that the object which they had approached with the intention of shooting was a man perfectly nude, but covered with a most remarkable growth of hair. The hair upon his head and his beard were very long, reaching to his waist; while his body, arms, and limbs were protected by the same natural covering. Hoping to approach and capture this strange being, they attempted to creep nearer; but he took alarm and rapidly ran away, jumping over bushes in his path like a deer. The two gentlemen decided to remain and camp in the same locality the second night, and they were again rewarded by a sight of the strange being. They were awakened in the night by a sound resembling that caused by striking flint upon steel and upon advancing in the direction of the sound they saw the same object, who appeared to be striking two flint rocks together. On their approach he again took alarm and ran away. We have heard reports of a wild man in that vicinity for several years past, but the gentleman who makes this statement is the only one that we have ever seen who vouches for the truth of the report. The gentleman is well known to us, and he asserted that he and his companion were willing to make oath to the truth of the statement.[10]

————————◆————————

Another large party started out yesterday to find the wild woman. They were out very nearly all day, but did not succeed in finding her, although they found fresh tracks.[11]

———————◆———————

THE WILD MAN OF YOLO

The wild man of Colusa and Yolo was again discovered one day last week near the county line. He was near a small lake, and wore nothing but a breechclout and the crown of a cap, acting in a strange manner, and dipping water from the lake with a can. He is about five and a half feet high, rather slim and his body is covered with hair nearly an inch long. His whiskers were ragged, and looked as if they had been haggled with sheep-shears. When he found he had been discovered, he ran into the tule and disappeared. Why does not some fortune-seeker capture that fellow and start a menagerie? The enterprise would doubtless prove remunerative, besides the people in the neighborhood of his rendezvous could spare him quite conveniently.[12]

———————◆———————

The "wild man" of Colusa and Yolo was again seen near Dunnigan's last week.[13]

———————◆———————

[1] *Santa Cruz Weekly Sentinel* (Santa Cruz, CA), September 15, 1866.

[2] *The Republican* (San Joaquin, CA), September 19, 1870.

[3] *Daily Transcript* (Oakland, CA), September 27, 1870.

[4] *Petaluma Weekly Argus* (Petaluma, CA), November 5, 1870.
Both this report and the previous, besides reading like many modern bigfoot reports whereupon tracks are found, followed by a sighting, include the witnesses reporting multiple creatures. This article in particular features a wonderful description of the creature as observed by the witness.

[5] *San Francisco Chronicle* (San Francisco, CA), January 20, 1871.

[6] *San Francisco Chronicle* (San Francisco, CA), January 6, 1872.

[7] *San Francisco Chronicle* (San Francisco, CA), August 31, 1873.

[8] *Los Angeles Herald* (Los Angeles, CA), October 4, 1873.
The term "lusus naturae" refers to a deformed person or animal. Whatever these fellows caught - and since Mr. Converse believes it to be a deformed bear my guess is it probably *was* a deformed bear - I do not believe it was a bigfoot creature - nor any of the "wild men" appearing in newspaper articles at the time. None of these reports note the wild men being bereft of arms or forelegs. In recent years, a black bear with missing forelegs from New Jersey made the news when someone filmed it walking upright through a residential neighborhood.

[9] *The Independent Record* (Helena, MT), April 25, 1876.
There are many modern bigfoot reports wherein a hunter relates that the creatures seem to understand what a gun is - or at least recognize that it is an instrument that can do harm. Here is another reported bigfoot behavior noted in the 19th as well as the 21st century.

[10] *Los Angeles Herald* (Los Angeles, CA), August 28, 1879.

[11] *Los Angeles Herald* (Los Angeles, CA), October 8, 1879.

[12] *The Petaluma Courier* (Petaluma, CA), October 8, 1879.

[13] *Los Angeles Herald* (Los Angeles, CA), October 26, 1879.

II. THE THING WAS OF GIGANTIC SIZE

CALIFORNIA 1881 - 1889

There is said to be a wild man in the woods near Campo.[1]

———————◆———————

The Bodie *Free Press* says they have a wild man in that neighborhood who has eyes like a cat, and every time he looks a man square in the face it has a bad effect.[2]

———————◆———————

A WILD MAN

———

The Strange Discovery Made by a Party in California.

While hunting for deserters from a ship at Guaymas, a few days ago, the searchers discovered a man covered from head to foot with long, shaggy hair, of a reddish color. On their approaching him he commenced to run, and they chased him, following him a distance of a mile or more to the beach, where he jumped from rock to rock with the agility of a chamois, and was soon lost to sight behind a jutting point. They afterward discovered the cave which he inhabits, the floor being covered with skins, and the indications were that he subsisted entirely upon raw fish. Organized efforts will be made to capture him.[3]

———————◆———————

A wild man has been seen in the willows in the vicinity of the Tule River bridge on the Bakersfield Road. He is presumed to be crazy. He lives on milk obtained from cows pastured in the valley and amuses himself by frightening a lone widow living in the neighborhood.[4]

———————◆———————

WILD MAN IN THE WOODS.

Residents in the neighborhood of the Collins ranch, adjoining the Scotia mine, just west of town, claim that a strange-looking wild man has for several weeks taken up his abode in the dense woods in that locality, and has made short visits to the farm-houses when pressed with hunger. On receiving food or being refused he invariably runs off with lightning speed to the woods. He is described as of middle age, and hardly any chin, wearing his tangled, matted hair down over his shoulders. Such clothing as he wears consists of tattered rags. His nails are long, like birds' claws, and he goes along with distorted features and mutterings as of one insane. He has been several times seen with a gunny sack on his shoulders, running like a wolf. He is supposed to have his abode in

one of the numerous tunnels that exist in the neighborhood.[5]

———————◆———————

— A genuine wild man of the woods has been troubling the farmers on the outskirts of Grass Valley.[6]

———————◆———————

The wild man recently reported as having been seen near New Westminster, B.C., is thought to be the same wild man who several months ago terrorized the residents in and about Grass Valley, Cal.[7]

———————◆———————

A wild man of the woods is scaring people in the neighborhood of the Big Bend mine in Butte County.[8]

———————◆———————

I do not remember to have seen any reference to the "Wild Man" which haunts this part of the country, so I shall allude to him briefly. Not a great while since, Mr. Jack Dover, one of our most trustworthy citizens, while hunting saw an object standing one hundred and fifty yards from him picking berries or tender shoots from the bushes.

The thing was of gigantic size — about seven feet high — with a bull dog head, short ears and long hair; it was also furnished with a beard, and was free from hair on such parts of its body as is common among men. Its voice was shrill, or soprano, and very human, like that of a woman in great fear. Mr. Dover could not see its footprints as it walked on hard soil. He aimed his gun at the animal, or whatever it was, several times, but because it was so human would not shoot. The range of the curiosity is between Marble Mountain and the vicinity of Happy Camp. A number of people have seen it and all agree in their descriptions except some make it taller than others. It is apparently herbivorous and makes its winter quarters in some of the caves of Marble Mountain. [9]

―――――― ◆ ――――――

A WILD MAN.

COTTONWOOD, December 19. — A school teacher from the east side of the river reports here that a wild or crazy man has appeared in Stillwater country and is creating a good deal of excitement by his strange actions. [10]

―――――― ◆ ――――――

A HAIRY WILD MAN

――――

Who Lives in the
Arroyo Honda and
Wears No Clothes.

SAN JOSE. February 27. — A wild man has been troubling ranchers near the mountains east of San Jose, in the Arroyo Honda, for several weeks past. It was first noticed that the frequent depredations of sheep occurred, and calves were killed and carried off. A few nights ago the man was seen and pursued by farmers to a cave in the mountain side apparently unapproachable. The pursuers could get no nearer than 500 yards of the cave. While being pursued the man uttered frightful shrieks. He has long hair and whiskers and his body is covered with hair and he wears no clothes. Sheriff Brower will go out in the morning and try to effect a capture. [11]

―――――― ◆ ――――――

DEAD-MAN'S HOLE

A TOUGH TALE OF NORTHERN SAN DIEGO COUNTY

The Adventure of Two Hunters with a Half-Human, Half-Animal Monster — The Mysterious Murders of That Section Explained.

The San Diego *Union* of Sunday contains a long account of a monster, half-human and half-animal, which had been killed at "Dead-Man's Hole," in the northeastern part of the county. The story is too long to reproduce entirely, but the following is the most interesting part of it:

Hunters seldom venture into Dead-Man's Hole, partly because of the general awe and fear of the place, but more especially because it is well known that there is no game there. Last Thursday, however, two venturesome hunters, named Edward Deau and Charles Cox, determined to explore the dark and mysterious canyon. After a hard struggle they had proceeded for about a mile through a tangled maze of brush and rocks. At each step the canyon became narrower and their progress was necessarily slower. Up to a certain point they had seen or heard nothing extraordinary, and the silence was quite oppressive when added to their natural fear of the mysterious place. The boulders and cuts in the canyon sides ahead of them were gradually becoming deeper and more impassable. The explorers had almost made up their minds to turn back, when suddenly they were startled by a slight rustle ahead of them, and almost immediately a crushing sound, as of some heavy object moving through the brush, was heard to proceed farther up the canyon.

The brush and rocks impeded the view, and the hunters scrambled up the canyon sides as quickly as they could to a commanding point. The sight that met their gaze almost paralyzed them with fear.

An immense, unwieldy animal, that from a rear view resembled a bear, was making rapid strides through the narrow dell. Its legs were long, and they were used with such ease and facility in climbing over the rocks and logs, that, on second thought, the animal appeared more like an immense gorilla. Its hair was dark brown, and it was at least six feet in height. The front legs, from their use, resembled arms, and the beast moved almost uprightly, like a man or monkey. Its body was quite round and covered with

14

extremely long hair, much unlike the hair of any animal. The hind legs, or feet, from the knees down, were the most peculiar features about the strange being. They were extremely broad and long, and the insides of them, upon which the animal walked, were entirely bare of hair. Every time it made a move it exposed to view the bottoms of its immense paws. Except for the hair, the arms and hands of the beast greatly resemble those of a human being. The body was large and round, and entirely devoid of a tail.

As soon as the hunters recovered from their surprise they began to follow the beast. It had no difficulty in moving along, and was making rapid headway up the canyon. To call its attention, and arrest its progress, Cox suddenly fired a pistol shot into the air. At the report the beast stopped and turned its face toward its pursuers. It was now about 20 yards distant, in full view, and terror was added to the surprise of the adventurers. They saw before them a human countenance. The animal turned almost instantly, and resumed its flight up the canyon.

The hunters were now more eager than ever in their pursuit. At last, the beast suddenly disappeared in a narrow, obscure cut, full of brush and fallen trees and immense boulders. The next moment it was seen scrambling toward a small opening in the rocky mountain side. At that instant, Cox, who is a wonderful shot with a rifle, brought his weapon to his shoulder and fired. With a cry like that of a human being, the beast instantly fell in a hideous heap across a boulder that it was in the act of scaling. Slowly and with much trepidation the hunters made their way to the prostrate object. It proved to be dead, shot through the breast. The face was exposed to view as it lay on its side on the rock. The features were unmistakable Indian in character. The hairs on the face were few and black, and on the head it was long and jet black, like that of an Indian. The skin of the face was very dark and wrinkled. The teeth, which were partially exposed by the position of the mouth, were plainly those of a carnivorous animal. They were longer than those of a human being. This was the only feature of the face and head that did not exactly resemble the characteristics of an Indian. Perhaps the most singular point about the strange creature was the disproportion between its head and body.

The former was not larger than that of an ordinary man, and yet the body would weigh 400 pounds. The long, muscular arms were provided with a pair of hands almost exactly like those of a man. There were five fingers on each hand. The outside of the fingers were covered in hair, but on the inside the skin was bare and white and thickly calloused in places. The feet, if such they could be called, were entirely unlike anything the hunters had seen. They were two feet long and eight inched broad, and covered on the bottom with a hard substance, like that of a dog. The being was of the male sex. It was evidently a cross between an Indian and some carnivorous animal. Such monstrosities, anthropologists say, are often born into the world, and many of them are mentioned in natural history.

After an examination of the body the hunters began an exploration of the opening toward which the animal was making its way. The entrance was under a large rock. The explorers advanced with caution, for fear of meeting the mate of the brute. A large apartment was found not more than 10 feet from the outside. It had evidently been dug out of the hard earth by hand. In the dim light it could be seen that the room was empty. Cox struck a match and by its blaze all the mysteries surrounding the murders in Dead-Man's Hole were revealed. In one corner was a pile of bones, among which were portions of human skeletons. Five human skulls were lying together. The half-man and half-beast was evidently also a semi-cannibal. On the floor, in the middle of the cave, was the half-devoured remains of a goat. In another corner of the room was a pile of leaves and weeds the animal used as a bed. These and the bones were the only objects in the cave.

The methods of the brute in its murderous work are evident. It sprang on its victims from behind and choked them to death. Then it would drag them to a place of concealment till nightfall. There is no doubt that if the bodies of Blair and Belita had not been found on the day they were murdered, they would never again have been heard of, as was the case with the many other mysterious disappearances in the Hole. The absence of human footprints or human motives, and all the other remarkable circumstances surrounding these murders, are now explained.[12]

———————◆———————

Thomas Cunningham, the sheriff of San Joaquin County, passed through the city yesterday, having been in San Diego in a chase for a wild man, whom he failed to capture.[13]

———————◆———————

— A wild man is reported to be roaming the woods above the Powder Works.[14]

———————◆———————

A WILD MAN

———

The Terror That Is Haunting the Woods of Santa Cruz.

Santa Cruz is wild with excitement, and the Santa Cruz small boy, and the Santa Cruz sport, and the Santa Cruz shot are all talking about the wild man in the woods somewhere near the powder works, with a good deal of apprehension. It is true, there is a "wild man" in the woods. A sort of horrible man, about six feet six inches in height, diaphonously arrayed and armed with a stout club. This man has been seen by teamsters and others, and last Saturday he attacked and almost killed an unfortunate woodsman. Several parties have volunteered their services to go out and search the woods for this awful man, and though Sunday is a day when most people are exempt from work, the bravest of the men could not find the leisure or muster up sufficient courage to go out and discover the disturber of the county's peace. He is said to be opposite the powder mills.

There is no more romantic sight in all the state than about here. The works lie in a small valley through which runs a small stream. The country is heavily wooded, and on the first ridge of the western cliff runs a railroad track. On the opposite side stands the beautiful home of the Superintendent of the powder works. It is a large white house, surrounded by flower beds and has a most superb view. The wild man is supposed to be hidden in these woods. The people about there are in a high degree of nervousness, as this man is said to be very dangerous. There are lots of theories about him. One is that he escaped from the insane asylum at Agnews, and that he will have to be shot before he can be captured. The excitement can be better imagined than described when it is said that these woods are a favorite resort for picnickers. The wild man, however, has chased all such ideas of enjoyment out of the minds of the people who think about having any such fun.

There is one slight inaccuracy in the above article which we wish to correct, and that is the height of the Santa Cruz wild man. The last man who saw him says that he is sixteen feet high, red haired, and wild eyed.[15]

———————◆———————

— The alleged wild man was seen by two boys at 4 a.m. Thursday seated on some ties on the railroad switch near the Powder Works. When he saw the boys he ran away.[16]

———————◆———————

Is It a Wild Man? — Is Catalina Still Inhabited by Natives? — A Yarn; Not of Fish.

A curious story was told here today that has excited no little interest among the editors of *The Jew Fish*, all being somewhat taken down at the fact that none of them invented this last story.

The yarn is that a goat-hunter came in yesterday, pale and frightened. As he was riding down the slope of Silver Canyon late in the afternoon a man, dark and hairy, dressed in skins, and armed with a stone club, dashed out of a cave and made for him. The goat-hunter put spurs to his horse and both went down the canyon at railroad speed, the wild man — he of the hair — leaping from rock to rock like a goat. When the hunter reached the bottom he turned and saw the wild man making off and sent a bullet after him, heard a terrible cry and then fled. The goat-hunter was sober, so it is said, and not subject to what is known as the "James Preserves," this sounding a little better than plain "Jim Jam." He is convinced that this is one of the survivors of the old Catalina race, perhaps the last one, and states that he was seven feet tall and a giant in every way. The earthquake shock felt at Los Angeles and Avalon at 6:15 last night was the reverberation caused by leaps of the wild man down hill. These things are all very simple when understood. The wild man is going to be captured, and a party is being formed from the Metropole to capture him, and if successful, he will be exhibited in number six of the hotel.

The editor of *The Jew Fish* is going out tomorrow to discover the cave in which the monster lives, the stone ornaments, the gold trinkets, weapons, etc., all of which will be exhibited at Avalon, for the benefit of science. That the wild man had a hairless dog, is evident, as the writer ran across a cave some time ago, and upon crawling in, a dead dog, dry as a chip, was found resting upon a stone. Whether this was the wild man's pet dog, or whether the wild man lived on dogs, or whether this dog was a howlless sacrifice at the wild man's altar, is not known. The expedition is going out, and developments are anxiously waited for by the scientific world.[17]

———————◆———————

[1] *The Record-Union* (Sacramento, CA), May 14, 1881.

[2] *The Petaluma Courier* (Petaluma, CA) July 27, 1881.

[3] *Sunday News*, (Wilkes-Barre, PA) June 25, 1882.

[4] *The Fresno Republican*, (Fresno, CA) April 28, 1883.
As strange as it may sound, in my previous collection of wild man stories, *Bigfoot in Pennsylvania*, there were other reports of bigfoot creatures milking cows. One report had the creatures suckling directly from the bovines. That said, this report may have referred to a human but the fact that whatever-it-was was getting milk from cows does not, in my view, eliminate the possibility that it could have been a bigfoot creature.

[5] *The Record-Union* (Sacramento, CA), December 7, 1883.
Another report in which the wild man in question may indeed be a regular human. However, there were just enough strange details - the bird-like claws, strange mutterings, and his running like a wolf - to warrant inclusion here.

[6] *Oakland Tribune* (Oakland, CA), December 10, 1883.

[7] *San Francisco Chronicle* (San Francisco, CA), February 19, 1884.

[8] *The Los Angeles Times* (Los Angeles, CA), March 24, 1885.

[9] *Del Norte Record* (Del Norte, CA), January 2, 1886.

[10] *San Francisco Chronicle* (San Francisco, CA), December 20, 1886.

[11] *Oakland Tribune* (Oakland, CA), February 27, 1888.

[12] *The Los Angeles Times* (Los Angeles, CA), April 8, 1888.
An amazing account which reads like so many modern bigfoot reports. Note first the eerie silence in the canyon before the hunters saw the creature. This silence is reported both preceding and during many, many bigfoot sightings. What follows thereafter is a stunning description of a bigfoot body, up close and personal, with so many details which we likewise hear from modern witnesses that it is almost like a checklist. From the soles of the feet (with rough pads like a dogs); to the locomotion of the creature (they could see the bottoms of its feet as it walked); to the barrel-chested body; the face with somewhat Native American features; the long arms; and large teeth - as incredible as it

sounds, it seems like these hunters really did kill a bigfoot creature given all of the details they report.

Deadman's Hole, was an isolated hollow with two spring-fed ponds at its mouth. Over the years, many dead bodies had turned up around Deadman's Hole - it seems the place earned its name - but in 1888 at least seven corpses were found in the area. Many of these were brutally strangled. If the hunters in this article are to be believed, it seems likely the bigfoot creature was killing and possibly eating humans. (Deadman's Hole information comes from *Death Alley*, an article in the *San Diego Reader* from August 4, 2010.)

[13] *The Daily Courier* (San Bernardino, CA), June 22, 1888.

[14] *Santa Cruz Sentinel* (Santa Cruz, CA), July 16, 1889.

[15] *Santa Cruz Sentinel* (Santa Cruz, CA), July 19, 1889.

[16] *Santa Cruz Sentinel* (Santa Cruz, CA), July 19, 1889.

[17] *Los Angeles Herald* (Los Angeles, CA), August 30, 1889.

Some other things, besides the details of bigfoot reports, do not change. Here we have a sarcastic tone and an attempt at humor by a reporter in 1889. More often than not any modern coverage of bigfoot in the mainstream press will include sarcasm and jokes - often at the expense of the witnesses. I believe certain reporters want to appear intelligent and "scientific" and throwing jokes and sarcasm into a story about bigfoot is their way to let the readers know they are "above" such nonsense without actually stating their views or confronting the witness with their opinions.

III. AN UNHEARD OF MONSTROSITY

CALIFORNIA 1890 - 1898

A Wild Man

The wild man whom several parties have attempted to capture was encountered in Lee Vining Creek Canyon last week by John Forsee. The man was clad from head to foot in coyote skins and wore round Indian snow-shoes. Though apparently quite aged, his hair and beard being white, he was agile as a deer and climbed the steep side of the canyon with incredible swiftness, giving vent occasionally to cries of fear. It is some years since we heard of this wild creature being seen, but he is doubtless the same who terrorized tourists in the early part of the present decade, when he distinguished himself by snatching a young lady from a mule in the presence of her companions and disappearing in the thick timber at the southwestern base of Mount Dana, evincing herculean strength and wonderful agility. She was found by a search party next day in a half demented condition, unable to give a lucid account of her experience, but no trace of her abductor could be discovered.[1]

————————◆————————

A WILD MAN

Belief that It Is Murderer Sim Welling

Twenty young men of Williams and vicinity went to the mountains recently for a few weeks' recreation. They pitched their camp on the east side of Snow Mountain, where Paradise Creek plunges down the green walled mountainside, while they lured the shy trout, the innocent deer and the fierce bear from their haunts in the unbroken mountain fastness. The boys enjoyed the allurements of the wilderness, and the wild game furnished their table with an abundance of the most delicate viands. During the evenings when all were about the campfire they at various times paused the telling of mirthful tales, thinking they had heard an intruding footstep near the camp. At last, however, in the middle of the night, when all was still about the place and wrapped in slumber, one of the young men was awakened by an unusual noise, and upon opening his eyes vision rested for a minute on the face of a strange man, whose beard and hair were unkempt, hatless and in tattered clothing. As soon as the stranger found that he was observed he disappeared into the fastness of the jungle.

There was no more sleep for the young man although he remained in his bed. In about two hours the strange figure returned, his long hair floating in the midnight breezes, his chin resting almost on his sunken chest, his bony fingers bent like a cat's paw when about to spring, and from his eyes shone an unnatural light. Breathless did the young man, who had the day before bravely faced an enraged bear, watch the approaching figure, whose countenance looked ghost-like in the light of the moon. The strange man approached the improvised table of the camp, where meat and bread from the last meal remained, and he ate ravenously, more like a wild beast than a human being. Presently the young man saluted him with a friendly greeting. Had an electric shock passed through his system he could not have acted more quickly. In an instant the wild man, for such he really appeared, sprang up the almost impassable mountainside as fleet as a deer. Excited and hardly knowing what he did the young denizen of the plains, who had conquered many a fair heart and broken scores of fractious mules, sent a rifle ball in the direction of the departing man. Hardly had the smoke of the gun cleared away when great boulders came rolling down the precipitous side of the mountain, evidently loosened by the wild being which had passed up.

The boys from that on lost their appetite for the juicy venison and delicate trout. They only remained a day or so after, but during that time the strange figure was often seen skulking near the camp like a wild animal, but invariably upon being discovered he would swiftly disappear into the most impenetrable jungle.

The description of this "wild man of the hills" tallies exactly with that of Sam Welling, who murdered Safford near Willows three years ago. It is presumed that it is the murderer, who escaped and went into the mountains, and that his crime, ever eating at his mind, together with the loneliness and hardships of such a life, drove him insane.[2]

———◆———

A wild woman has been seen in the foothills, near Madera, by several stockmen. They have tried to catch her with lassos, but she scales rocks as easy as a goat.[3]

———◆———

A FRESNO FREAK

———

A Wild Woman Said to Live in the Mountains.

There has been considerable excitement at the mountain mills recently over the repeated appearance of a reported wild woman. The strange creature has been seen frequently roaming the forests, and on any attempt to capture her flees to the rocks where she recklessly leaps from crag to crag and manages to elude her pursuers. She occasionally visits the eating house at the mill and begs something to eat from the Chinese cook. It is said that the woman, or whatever it may be, has been seen at night with a dark lantern several times.

One night two employees were walking from the mill to the logging camp, and at a lonely part of the road they were suddenly covered by a bright light, which was suddenly vanished. To say they were scared is putting it mildly, and they did some tall amateur sprinting to get out of that region. There were several repetitions of the dark-lantern performance, and the supposed wild woman was recognized as the wielder of the lantern. Several who have seen the creature are disposed to believe it is a crazy man dressed in woman's clothes. Constable Merritt and a posse from Fresno Flats have gone to the mountains with the avowed intention of capturing the "what is it."[4]

------◆------

WHAT IS IT?

An Unheard of Monstrosity Seen in the Woods.

Mr. Smith, a well known citizen of northern Capay Valley, called on us today and tells us the following strange story which we would be loth to believe if it were not for the fact that he is an old acquaintance of this office, and has always borne a spotless reputation. Several days ago, Mr. Smith together with a party of hunters, were above Ramsey hunting. One morning Mr. Smith started out early in quest of game, he had not gone far when his attention was attracted by a peculiar noise that seemed to come from an oak tree that stood nearby. Looking up Mr. Smith was startled to see gazing at him what was apparently a man clothed in a suit of shaggy fur. Having heard of wild men, Mr. Smith was naturally placed upon his guard, but thinking that he would see "what virtue there was in kindness," he called to the supposed man to come down, as he was filled with nothing but the kindest motives. This speech did not have the desired effect, rather the opposite, for the strange thing gave grunts of unmistakable anger. Believing that discretion was the better part of valor, our informant stood not upon the honor of his going, but went at once in a bee-line for the camp. After placing some distance between himself and the strange creature, the hunter turned around just in time to see it descend the tree. Upon reaching the ground, instead of standing upright as a man would, it commenced to trot along the ground as a dog or any other animal would do.

Mr. Smith describes the animal as being about six feet high when standing, which it did not do perfectly, but bent over, after the manner of a bear. Its head was very much like that of a human being. The trapezoid muscles were very thick and aided much in giving the animal its brutal look. The brow was low and contracted, while the eyes were deep set, giving it a wicked look. It was covered with long shaggy hair, except the head, where the hair was black and curly.

Mr. Smith says of late sheep and hogs to a considerable extent have disappeared in his vicinity and their disappearance can be traced to the hiding place of the "What Is It." Among those who have suffered are Henry sharp, Jordan Sumner, Herman Laird and J.O. Trendle.

Here is a chance for some energetic young man to start a dime museum and acquire a fortune within a very few years. Anyone wishing to learn more about this peculiar monstrosity can do so by calling on our informant who will no doubt take a delight in piloting them to the dangerous vicinity of the late scene of action.[5]

———————◆———————

WOODLAND'S WONDER

———

A Strange Creature, Supposed to be a Gorilla.

WOODLAND, April 10. — It is reported today that a strange creature much resembling a gorilla has been seen in the hills adjacent to Capay Valley. The story is vouched for by more than one responsible man. It is said to be at least six feet tall when standing erect, travels on all fours, climbs trees and has wonderful strength in his hands. It has a shaggy covering. Much interest is excited over the find of this "what is it?" and an effort is

to be made to learn more concerning it.[6]

———————◆———————

John and Dave Lowry were down from Rumsey Saturday. They say the strange and mysterious animal still sojourns in that vicinity and has frequently been seen by hunters. Many sheep have lately been devoured in the locality and the depredations are attributed to the "What-is-It." It is generally believed that the daring intruder is nothing more or less than a gorilla. It will be remembered that some time last fall a circus train was wrecked and burned up north and many of the animals escaped. Among the number was a gorilla and it is thought the animal has followed down the Coast and is now the object of so much curiosity in the neighborhood of Rumsey.[7]

———————◆———————

THE "WHAT IS IT?"

———

Still At Large and Devouring Everything Within its Wake.

———

We have received a communication from Mr. James

E. Martin of Casey's Flat, giving us additional information regarding the strange animal seen in that vicinity some weeks ago. Mr. Martin is one of the best known citizens of this county and is well known in this city, at present he is homesteading a quarter section above Rumsey. Much of his spare time Mr. Martin spends in trapping, and of course if anyone would know anything of the "wild man of the woods" it would be him.

But to his story: About the sixth of this month, some of Mr. Martin's horses strayed from his premises. While out looking for them, he suddenly came across a trail showing that some kind of dead animal had been dragged through the brush. The gentleman's curiosity was excited at such a large animal being made away with, so he followed it as fast as the jagged rocks and matted brush would allow him. Proceeding slow and cautiously, with keen eyes and steady nerves, he felt as though he was about to have a hand encounter with the beast that had done the killing. After going some distance, he came upon the partly devoured remains of a two-year-old heifer, which he recognized as the property of Mr. John W. Clapp. After the monster had satisfied himself on a large portion of the flesh, he had covered the dead carcass over with brush and dirt

and had departed. Mr. Martin measured the tracks of the beast, and found them to be sixteen inched long and eight inched broad, with long claws, with which it had torn up the earth that covered the slain heifer.

Our informant is not a coward by any means, but he suddenly remembered he always felt better about that time of day if he had his trusty Winchester with him, so, making his way homeward, he took his gun, and mounting a horse, proceeded to Mr. Clapp's, where he told him what he had seen. Mr. Clapp returned with him, and together they proceeded to the spot. To say that Mr. Clapp was grieved at the loss of his fine bovine, now torn limb from limb, would be putting it mildly.

Late that night, as Mr. Martin lay asleep, he was aroused by the piteous whines of his dogs, which are blood thirsty and ferocious animals. On opening the door, the dogs rushed in and skulked under the bed, where they shivered with fright and fear, and from which place they could not be driven either by threats or entreaties. Stepping outside to see what was the matter, Mr. Martin heard something moving away from his cabin, at the same time giving vent to some most unearthly screams that echoed from crag to mountain, and which finally died away in the lonely canyons. The gentleman asks for aid in capturing this unknown creature, and says that if he can but secure the necessary help, he will not stop until he has captured it dead or alive.

Here is a chance for some of our local braves to make a name for themselves.[8]

———————◆———————

People around here are afraid to travel the roads above here after sunset for fear of meeting the "What Is It" or getting struck by a meteor. Very likely this valley will be uninhabited in a few years, as strange monsters and falling bodies are getting more numerous and bolder each day, and footprints of the monster are now seen as far down the creek as Madison.[9]

———————◆———————

A WILD MAN IN THE SINK.

———

From what meager reports we can secure it seems that a wild man has taken up his abode in the sink of Cache Creek. Just who the fellow is, or how he came there, no one seems to know. He is described as being something over six feet tall, and weighing about two hundred pounds. His hair, which is light in color, reached almost to his waist. He is very shy, and when approached seems inclined to keep out of the way, although he will not flee as if in fright.

A few days ago one of our local hunters was out in the thicket, and to his surprise came upon a beaten path that showed naked human footprints. He knew that they could not be that of a lady, unless she hailed from Chicago, and guessing at once that a wild man or something of that kind might be about, he pushed his way carefully through the underbrush, and had gone but a few paces when he came upon a "wickup" of the rudest make that would keep off the wind. A hasty search showed some rude cooking materials. The sight of a club standing nearby, partially covered with blood, tended to shorten the call.

People in that part of the county say that so far he has been harmless, and they have no complaint to make of their odd neighbor.[10]

———————◆———————

The wild man competition is now raging with the usual summer madness. Cache Creek, Yolo County, made the first bid with a 200-pounder, with red hair four feet long and a bloody club, and now Fresno, grown tired of its petrified person, produces a hairy what is it dressed in skins, ugly enough to scare a Chinese sheepherder. The wild man is a summer animal, and no doubt sucks his paws all winter.[11]

———————◆———————

"THE WHAT IS IT"

Seen Once More — It Has Not Reformed Yet.

Once more the wild and wooly "What Is It" has been seen. It does not seem to have reformed as yet, as it is as frisky as ever. This time the person who saw it was a Mr. Herman Gilbert, who was up in the head of Capay Valley looking for a suitable piece of government land that he might homestead.

He says that he was near Rumsey, where he was stopping with some friends. On last Monday morning he started out with his brother-in-law, expecting to be gone a day or so, as he wished to combine business with pleasure. They came to a nice little valley about a half mile long on Tuesday afternoon, and as it was cool, well watered and full of nice green grass, they determined to pitch their tent there. This they did, and about half an hour later Mr. Gilbert went to the spring nearby to water the horses, and was surprised to see around it tracks very much resembling that of a man, but thought nothing of it. Incidentally, when he returned, he mentioned it to his brother-in-law. He then, for the first time, heard of the terror, and suggested that the two return and track the mysterious animal to his lair. This they did, and as they followed the footprints, they found that they led to the other end of the valley. Just as they came to the end of the defile and were about to turn down the mountainside, they heard a peculiar cry, half human and half brutish, and quite near them. As may be supposed, they wended their way very carefully and slowly. Before they had gone half a mile, they came upon a path. The gentlemen were too sharp to walk in it, and followed the direction it took by walking in the underbrush nearby.

Just as they reached the bottom of the mountain, they came into a deep ravine and there, walking up and down, could be seen "his nibs" himself. Mr. Gilbert says that the beast seemed to be mad at something, and would beat its breast, which was covered with gore, and the sound made thereby was like distant thunder. It had lost some hair since last seen, so the gentleman should judge, for the cuticle was plainly discernible and was of a dark color, much like that of a horse.

Nearby was a rude cave where the anomaly lived. About it could be seen bones from which the flesh had been eaten. The stench arising from the decaying matter was horrible. The muscles of the creature were very powerful, and the creature made an exhibition of its strength once by lifting a huge rock that would weigh at least three hundred pounds and throwing it, without any apparent effort, a hundred feet.

After watching the "What Is It" for some time the gentlemen crept quietly back, and as soon as possible left the locality, determined not to make acquaintance with the Capay curiosity.[12]

———————◆———————

THE CAPAY MONSTER

———

It Turns Out to be Only a Wild and Wooly Jackass.

Some weeks ago various stories were published concerning a strange monster which was said to be roaming the canyons north of Capay Valley, and some thrilling tales were told of its doings. The Woodland *Mail* thus explains:

"At last there seems to be a satisfactory explanation offered of the mysterious animal that has so long been the terror to not only the nervous old maids and timorous damsels of fair Capay, but also of the brave stalwart males of that section. When we state on the authority of E.B. Aldrich that the strange beast is nothing more than a small Maltese jack the nervous tension of the valley of the fig and olive will doubtless relax. Now, it is said that this jack, which is only about the size of a large dog, is one of the most voracious quadrupeds in the world, and as to his lungs — great heavens, when he brays it is said that the echo of his hypochondriac roar reverberates through the melancholy stillness of Cache Creek Canyon like unto the doleful undulations of maddened thunder.

"Notwithstanding his terrorizing roar, however, his Maltese highness is not now considered dangerous to human life, though he has been known to gormandize on a full fledged calf for breakfast, with a few tender lambs for dessert, and was turned at large some time ago from Casey Flat because of his diabolical inclination to chase men out of his corral. There may be some mistake about the stories of him climbing trees, though it is quite likely that if he ever started to make one of his meals from an ordinary oak tree he would reach the top before his appetite became satiated."[13]

———————◆———————

A wild man roams the hills near Niles and frightens the children.[14]

———————◆———————

THE WILD MAN OF CAPAY

An Individual Who is Creating Alarm in That Neighborhood.

The people of Capay, says the Woodland *Mail*, are excited over the strange and unaccountable actions of a man who is thought to be either crazy or wild. He has been seen frequently in the hills about Capay, but whenever he finds he is seen he runs into the brush and gets out of sight.

The other night Ben Duncan, who lives about two miles above Capay, was aroused by the fierce barking of dogs, and went to the door just in time to see the strange individual scaling the yard fence. He is known to have visited and broken into several houses lately, but his only object seems to be to procure something to eat. Constable Moore and others have been scouring the hills, but have been unable to get close enough to capture him, although he is frequently seen. Neither has anyone been able to obtain any description of him, further than he appears to be a medium-sized man.

The belief prevails with many that it is Wohlfrom, who has either become demented or is hiding about and waiting under fear of venturing further. But it is nothing more than mere supposition, as there are no grounds for basing such a theory upon. But the people of the neighborhood are thoroughly aroused, and it is likely that his capture will be effected before long.[15]

———————◆———————

One is tempted to class among freaks the two dozen "messiahs" who, during the year, have made their appearance in this country and elsewhere; but the genus "wild man" claims a little attention. It is noticeable that twenty wild men have been found in the United States in the twelve months just passed. The weird story of the wild man of Fresno was published very fully in the Chronicle, and an uncanny yarn it was indeed. A naked human being with matted hair, flaming eyes and limbs gnarled with muscles who haunted a few veracious woodsmen and scared them "out of their wits," using their own words. Woodland also discovered a gorilla that seemed half man, at least. The Denver "Homo," who lived on roots and studied theosophy was a notable find of this sort.[16]

————————◆————————

An alleged wild man keeps children in the northern part of Marin County in a state of terror.[17]

————————◆————————

PLACER'S WILD MAN

————

A Bear River Hermit Who is Not on the Register.

————

Almost Naked and Wild as a Deer — Strange Discovery Made by Some Boys.

————

The Placer *Herald* of Saturday tells the following interesting story: "A gentleman by the name of S. Noman was in town the other day and told a rather sensational story about a wild man, who has been discovered out near Bear River, in this county, in the wooded region between Gautier's and the McCourtney Crossing. His den was first found by some boys who were out on foot after cattle. On the south side of Bear River, at a point where the bank consists of large boulders for some distance up the side of the canyon, there is one place where rocks the size of houses have so lodged as to form a natural cavern. The boys in climbing over the rocks saw the opening and concluded to explore it.

"As they neared the place they noticed in the bottom of a small ravine leading to the cave evidences of a trodden path and the plain signs of human footprints. This further excited their curiosity, and they concluded that some Indians had been occupying the place temporarily. On reaching the opening they were further surprised to find, a short distance from the mouth, the live embers of a smoldering fire. Bones were numerous near the cave, and on a ledge of rock rested about half of a small-sized hog which had been dressed by skinning. Well back in the cave was a lot of old sacks, rags and leaves, so impressed as to indicate that they had been used for a bed. All the signs showed that the occupant or occupants were human, and that the place had not been long deserted.

"They got to speculating as to what might happen if the owners, whatever it, he, she, or they might be, should find them there. They prudently concluded to retire a short distance and from behind a pile of rocks where the cave could be seen by them watch a while at least for developments. With this idea in view they started to climb over the rocks, but had not gone more than fifty yards when they were startled by an unearthly screech followed immediately by the whizzing of a rock past their heads. They turned, and looking in the direction whence came the noise they saw standing on a large flat rock about seventy-five yards distant, and on the farther side of the cave from them a veritable 'wild man of the woods' or a 'cave-dweller of the foothills.' He hurled rocks at them at such a lively rate that they found it necessary to take shelter behind the boulders, and by dodging from one to another they soon got away.

"They describe him as stalwart in form, bronzed in color, naked except some rags or skins around his loins, and hair rough, ragged, and hanging to his shoulders. The boys reported their discovery, and the neighborhood, as may be supposed, has become considerably excited, and while everybody is anxious to know more of the strange cave dweller, there are few who care to take the responsibility of visiting his habitation. There is talk of organizing an expedition for the purpose of thoroughly investigating the case and capturing the wild creature.

"The loss of many a pig and calf, the mysterious disappearance of which has been the cause of ugly suspicions among the neighbors, is now accounted for, and the feeling in that section is that the wild man must be captured or driven away, or the people there continue to stand the loss of such of their animals as he wants to eat. Who the man is or where he came from nobody in the neighborhood seems to know. His appearance and the signs about his habitation indicate that he has been there a long time."[18]

————————◆————————

A WILD MAN

———

He is Turned Up
This Time in Santa Rosa

Al Hutchings, an employee at Markham's Mill, discovered a wild man last Monday that is more than a match for the one Sheriff Mulgrew unearthed a year ago. Hutchings was strolling leisurely in the bushes about two miles from the mills when he heard a crackling sound proceeding from a clump of live oaks. He thought it was a bear and stood for a few seconds with his rifle ready to get a shot at the supposed bruin when it emerged from the covering. When the creature did make its appearance it presented a sight that made Hutchings' hair stand on end. It was nothing more or less than a human being, having a wild, maniacal look and covered down to the knees with a growth of long and shaggy hair. Hutchings stood as if rooted to the spot. The weird-looking creature strode or half-leaped out into the clearing and looked about as if fearing someone was near. Being evidently satisfied that there were no intruders in the vicinity, the wild man gave vent to a deep, guttural sigh and seated himself on his haunches. During this time Hutchings cautiously retired behind a neighboring tree, from which point of vantage he obtained a complete view of the freak. Hutchings states that the wild man was about 5 feet 8 or 9 inches in height. The hair which fell from his head was fully two feet long, very matted and of a reddish hue. His face was scantily covered with a beard of a sandy color.

From the shoulders to the knees a thick hirsute growth covered the body to such an extent that it appeared as if the man wore a woolen garment, so effectually did it cover his person. After squatting on his haunches for a few minutes the strange specimen of humanity stretched himself out for a nap in the blazing sunlight. Fearing to rouse the wild man to active hostilities were he to make his presence known, Hutchings quietly slipped away, leaving the strange son of Adam to enjoy his repose in peace. No one living in the vicinity of Markham's has ever seen the man before.

From Hutchings description, the wild man is about 40 years of age. It is supposed that he is the same individual who startled the country in the vicinity of Gualala about eight years ago by his sudden and unexpected debut. It is believed that he is an escaped lunatic who has long been given up as dead. Hutchings and three men intend to search the country and capture the human freak, if they can do so without taking his life.[19]

———————◆———————

Prairie City is excited over a wild-man scare, and the shepherds are all reported to be leaving the ranges at the back of town. Nobody seems to be able to supply a minute description of the ogre.[20]

———————◆———————

Wild Man of the Desert

SAN BERNARDINO, Feb. 18. — John Wilson Williamson, a mining man, reports the discovery of a wild man on the desert, four miles below Chuck Warren's ranch in the Big Moronogo Pass. The freak bears evidence of having lived underground and was extremely difficult to approach.[21]

———————◆———————

It is reported that a wild man is running at large on Grand Island. It is said that a resident of Arbuckle gave him a close chase on horseback a few days ago, but failed to capture him.[22]

———————◆———————

THAT JABBERWOCK

———

A Kern County Journalist Tells What It Is

The author of the frozen man, the pterodactyl, and the tree climbing clam stories has "got in his work again," and regales *The Fresno Republican* with a blood curdling account of some strange, uncouth creature that is ranging the wilds of that county. This wonderful animal "resembles a human being, beats his breast with long, powerful arms, and gives utterance to loud, guttural roars that make the air shiver as well as the spectators."

The probabilities are that Bully Foote and Eugene Deuprey are taking their summer outing in the mountains, and have been seen by some frightened campers who are not acquainted with the court room manners of those gentlemen. [23]

———————◆———————

The "Wild Man of Borneo" has been found in Kern County, near the headquarters of Muta Creek in the Alamo Mountains, about sixty miles south of this city and some thirty miles southeast of San Emigdio. The fellow is reported as in rags and tatters and having a beard reaching below his waist. He is as timid as a deer, leaps around like a cat with her head in a pitcher, and is very speedy.[24]

———————◆———————

Colfax has a sensation in the shape of a "wild man" roving the woods thereabouts.[25]

———————◆———————

Farmers living near Grayson are wrought up over the presence of a so-called wild woman in that vicinity. She sleeps in barns or haystacks. Her clothing is said to be worn to shreds and her feet are bare. A party of men has gone in pursuit of the demented creature.[26]

———————◆———————

A wild man, who is said to be almost entirely nude, has been discovered roaming about the mountains west of Mayfield, his appearance striking terror into the souls of residents in the vicinity.[27]

———————◆———————

An Insane Woman Is Running Wild in the Neighborhood of Bells Station.

———

Eludes Searching Parties and Terrifies the Residents With Her Screams.

———

SAN JOSE, CA, Feb 12 — A wild woman is reported to be roaming at large in the vicinity of Bells Station, near Gilroy, and is causing considerable uneasiness among the farmers in that section.

The woman has been seen several times in Harpers Canyon, but when approached would run away, screaming at the top of her voice.

The authorities in that vicinity have been searching for the woman for two days, but have been unable to find her. The woman, who is a stranger in that section, is evidently insane.[28]

———————◆———————

SAW A WILD MAN

The Local Adventurer Who Returns with a "Story."

At Davidson's a man named Swett reported meeting a wild man a few days ago four or five miles from the camp, who was possessed of a ferocious aspect, long hair and beard, few clothes, and no doubt numerous devils. Neither of them having his card with him, they both felt embarrassed and departed very hastily in opposite directions.[29]

———————◆———————

SHE TRAVELS WITHOUT CLOTHES

Wild Woman Seen in Ione Woods.

Holds Up J.S. Amick and Wife at Their Horses' Heads.

He Grapples with Her, but She Froths and Flees.

IONE, Sept. 11 — For several days reports have been received here to the effect that a woman with long, black hair and piercing black eyes, had been seen in the woods above town entirely nude. The other evening about dusk, J.S. Amick and wife, while driving home, some three miles from here, encountered the woman, who sprang from the brush at the roadside and seized the bridles of their team.

Amick left the wagon and grappled with the stranger, who was frothing at the mouth and gave vent to fearful shrieks, but she broke away from him and escaped. A systematic search for the supposed maniac will be made with bloodhounds.[30]

———————◆———————

WILD MOUNTAIN MAN

Has Las Flores Canyon a wild man? This question confronted the men who are working on the Mount Lowe railroad today. Las Flores Canyon is the first canyon west of Rubio Canyon, and a wagon road runs up to the head of it. The canyon is a pretty one, being almost the only pretty one saved from the devastation of forest fires. It is a favorite place for picnickers. Today, shortly after dinner, two section hands from Rubio Canyon walked around to Las Flores. Near the mouth of the canyon they met two men in a buggy, who stopped them to state that there was a naked man, evidently crazy, a little outside the canyon. The two men started curiously in the direction indicated and found a middle-aged, slightly bald, smooth-faced, sandy-complexioned man of large proportions sitting on a rock under a small oak, about twenty feet from the roadside, along which vehicles pass quite frequently, there being some houses in the canyon. There was not a stitch of clothing on the man, not even shoes or hat. He held a garment in his lap and went through a senseless ceremony which reminded the onlookers of a monkey's antics. He kept up incessantly an incoherent monologue and hummed a tune. The two men from Rubio approached within a few paces, making enough noise to attract the attention of an ordinary mortal, but failed to arouse the freak. They debated whether to accost him, but concluded upon sizing up his gigantic muscular development, that, insane, they wished no business with him, and, sane, he evidently wished no business with them. So the two men went back to work without disturbing the stranger, but the mystery of the thing worries them, and they have spread some of its contagion to the town. Who is he? Perhaps some man who has been fighting fire, has become suddenly deranged by the heat and smoke and hardship, and is wandering about in search of his people. Perhaps he is an escapee from the asylum, or perhaps he is a harmless freak whose crankiness takes this peculiar turn.[31]

———————◆———————

[1] *The Times* (Philadelphia, PA), April 25, 1890.

Though the visual description of the wild-man in question may lead some to conclude that it was not a bigfoot creature, several features of this article caught my attention: the "herculean strength" and great agility evinced by the "wild man"; his ability to climb with "incredible swiftness"; and most disturbing of all, the abduction of the young woman. I have heard other accounts of women supposedly abducted by bigfoot creatures who, when found, were in a state of insanity and could not or would not give account of their abduction.

[2] *The San Francisco Call* (San Francisco, CA), September 19, 1890.

Perhaps Sam Welling was creeping around the camp, but he seems to have adapted many bigfoot behaviors in his years away from society.: slipping into camps at night; throwing or rolling huge boulders; observing campers from the shadows… and somehow Sam's eyes have started to shine with an "unnatural light". Sam sounds a lot like a bigfoot.

[3] *The San Francisco Call* (San Francisco, CA), December 1, 1890..

[4] *San Francisco Chronicle* (San Francisco, CA), December 4, 1890.

Some odd details in this story compelled me to include it here. Besides the "wild woman" leaping easily from rock to rock, and the fact that the article refers to her as a " strange creature" and a "what is it", there seems to be some activity involving unusual lights - here said to be her lantern.

[5] *Woodland Daily Democrat* (Woodland, CA), April 9, 1891.

[6] *San Francisco Chronicle* (San Francisco, CA), April 11, 1891.

[7] *Woodland Daily Democrat* (Woodland, CA), May 6, 1891.

In newspapers all over the country the "wrecked circus train" is offered as an explanation for sightings of upright-walking, hair-covered creatures. Very rarely do they mention a specific place where the train crashed. Very few circuses could even afford gorillas - the animals were extremely expensive, rare, and difficult to care for. There were not even enough gorillas in the United States at the time to account for all these supposed circus train crashes / gorilla escapes.

[8] *Woodland Daily Democrat* (Woodland, CA), May 13, 1891.

While Mr. Martin never lays eyes on the creature (at least in this article), here again we have so many features of modern bigfoot reports. The reaction of his canines alone is echoed again and again in bigfoot reports, new and old. Whatever these creatures are, many dogs seem to be terrified of them - and with good reason it seems as reportedly the creatures often kill our beloved canine best friends.

[9] *Woodland Daily Democrat* (Woodland, CA), June 3, 1891.
 I find it extremely interesting that meteors are noted here in the same area as the creature sightings. "UFO" just like "bigfoot" and "Sasquatch" would not have been a term used at this time. One wonders if the meteors were simply meteors.

[10] *Woodland Daily Democrat* (Woodland, CA), June 12, 1891.

[11] *Oakland Tribune* (Oakland, CA), June 18, 1891.

[12] *Woodland Daily Democrat* (Woodland, CA), June 25, 1891.

[13] *The Record-Union* (Sacramento, CA), August 1, 1891.
 Another feature of newspapers, modern and old, when reporting on bigfoot sightings is to offer "logical" explanations, no matter how ridiculous. I find the story of a meat-eating mule with a voracious appetite far more unbelievable than the stories of hairy bipeds walking around in the mountains and valleys of California. Never mind that a mule is simply not what any of the other witnesses reported seeing. It seems for many newspapers it only takes one person to offer up a common solution, no matter how far it differs from what witnesses have reported, to cancel out all of their observations, no matter how detailed and, in this case, un-mule-like they may be. I take great delight in finding, much of the time, articles which report creature sightings in the same area after the newspaper skeptics have "solved" the mystery. (See [15] below.)

[14] *The Petaluma Courier* (Petaluma, CA), August 5, 1891.

[15] *The Record-Union* (Sacramento, CA), December 18, 1891.

[16] *San Francisco Chronicle* (San Francisco, CA), January 10, 1892.
 An excerpt from a much larger article discussing "freaks" and oddities of all sorts that were reported in newspapers the year previous. This paragraph was the only part relevant to the topic at hand.

[17] *San Francisco Chronicle* (San Francisco, CA), March 30, 1892.

[18] *The Record-Union* (Sacramento, CA), April 18, 1892.
 The presence of a smoldering fire does not automatically eliminate this wild-man from the possibility of being a bigfoot,

especially in California. First Nations people have told stories about bigfoot creatures knowing how to use fire there, but avoiding it as it tends to give their location away. The "unearthly screech" and the rock throwing may point to a bigfoot here.

19 *San Francisco Call* (San Francisco, CA), June 27, 1892.

20 *Woodland Daily Democrat* (Woodland, CA), August 23, 1892.

21 *San Francisco Call* (San Francisco, CA), February 19, 1893.

22 *Woodland Daily Democrat* (Woodland, CA), July 24, 1893.

23 *The Fresno Weekly Republican* (Fresno, CA), August 4, 1893.

24 *Oakland Tribune* (Oakland, CA), October 19, 1893.

25 *Oakland Tribune* (Oakland, CA), February 10, 1893.

26 *San Francisco Chronicle* (San Francisco, CA), April 21, 1894.

27 *Santa Cruz Sentinel* (Santa Cruz, CA), June 15, 1894.

28 *San Francisco Call* (San Francisco, CA), February 13, 1896.

29 *The San Bernardino County Sun* (San Bernardino, CA), September 6, 1896.

30 *The Los Angeles Times* (Los Angeles, CA), September 12, 1896.

31 *The Los Angeles Herald* (Los Angeles, CA), August 27, 1898.

IV. DEMON YELLS
AND GUTTURAL HOWLS

CALIFORNIA 1900 - 1909

SAW THE WILD MAN

Adventure of Fred Birlem and Howard Martin in Marin County.

MOUNT TAMALPAIS, May 21. — Fred Birlem of 2005 Green Street, San Francisco, and Howard Morton, musical critic for several local journals, met with an adventure while camping on the mountainside Saturday night which effectively deprived them of their rest, and but for their presence of mind might have resulted seriously.

Birlem and Morton left San Francisco on Saturday night intending to ascend Mount Tamalpais and watch the sunrise on Sunday morning. When they had climbed some distance they decided to camp for awhile and resume the ascent when rested. Birlem was just dozing off when a crackling in the brush aroused him. He flashed on a club electric light he carried and its rays showed him a wild figure standing over him. He drew a pistol and the mysterious intruder turned and rushed down the mountainside yelling like a demon. Both young men think that they encountered the famous wild man of Tamalpais, but more skeptical friends say a marauding tramp caused their fright.[1]

WILD MAN'S LAIR
UP ON TAMALPAIS

Queer Find of Marin County Deputy Sheriff.

Cabin in a Gulch

Cleverly Built Shelter Abandoned by a Hermit.

SAN RAFAEL, July 28. — The lair of the famous wild man of Mount Tamalpais has in all probability been discovered by Deputy Sheriff Edward Watson, who is employed as a watchman on the mountain. Watson reports that he discovered by the merest accident a brush cabin in one of the brushiest and most inaccessible canyons of the mountain.

Some days ago while riding up the road he went out on a small ridge to get a better view of the country, when he noticed what appeared to be a well-beaten trail leading into the gulch. Tying his horse, he started to investigate. The trail zig-zagged in a bewildering manner for a considerable distance, then it led across and over a ledge of rocks, at the foot of which was a small flat, or bench, twenty or thirty feet square. Under a large mountain oak in the upper end of the clearing was a neatly built brush house, constructed something on the plan of an Indian basket. In the cabin was a rude bunk made of poles. It was covered with a layer of leaves and dirt to a depth of several inches. Watson's attention was immediately attracted to a large dirk knife, which had been drivin to its hilt in the covering and in the center of the bed. He carried this weapon away with him as a relic.

Lying scattered about the ground near the hut were many pieces of wearing apparel, they having evidently been cut or torn to shreds, a few old cans and feathers from bluejays and woodpeckers.

It is very unlikely that any hunter would locate in so inhospitable a place, and, besides, the variety of birds evidently killed or trapped by the occupant were not such as are usually considered edible.

Some months ago rumors of a wild man on the mountain were current, but they were generally disbelieved. The present find of Watson gives color to the story. If the wild man still lives he has certainly removed his hiding place to some more secluded nook.[2]

43

---◆---

WILD MAN AGAIN

The old story of a naked wild man covered with a thick growth of hair from head to foot, comes from McKitrick. Such an individual yesterday attacked James Richardson and a companion while they were staking out oil claims. The fight was fast and furious while it lasted, but Richardson wrenched a rusty musket out of the lunatics hands, used it as a club, and drove him away. The wild man put off for the desert hills and the others came to town for the services of a doctor. Each had a number of scratches, and Richardson is severely injured in the back.[3]

---◆---

Ranchers of the Sur district, about 40 miles south of Monterey, CA, have been greatly disturbed of late over the frequent appearance of a wild man, who frightens women and children, and steals food from the pantries of the farmhouses. During the past few weeks a number of sheep have been killed and skinned by him, and portions of meat from the hind quarters cut away. Poultry has been stolen and even provisions from the houses. He goes about unclad, except for a scant tunic of sheepskin, and his unkempt hair and beard fly wildly about as he runs. He appears at all hours of the day and night, but never takes anything except food. He never speaks, and if spoken to or approached he disappears with marvelous swiftness into the brush.[4]

---◆---

Why don't the Chutes managers take a pack of bloodhounds and capture the Wild Man of Arroyo Seco and put him on exhibition with the other freaks?[5]

---◆---

WILD MAN REAPPEARS

After an absence of four years from his haunts, "the wild man of the Cienegitas" has again made his appearance, and is terrifying those who are obliged to pass the lonely strip of Hollister Avenue opposite the Sisters' Ranch. By those who have seen him he is described as a man of medium height, with long hair and beard, perfectly nude, and inhabiting the thick underbrush that fills the swamp on the west side of the avenue. A few days ago, a lady residing at La Patera was driving along that part of the road after nightfall, when he ran and caught the horse by the bridle. Between the vigorous use of the whip in the lady's hand, and the fight of the horse, which started to run, the lady made her escape. He never has been known to put in his appearance when a man accompanies a lady. Numerous attempts to catch him have been made with no success, the thick growth of willows and wild vines affording an excellent hiding place.[6]

a short distance away. Before he could attack the defenseless woman, Babcock shot at him again, when the stranger turned and fled into the brush.

That night the wild man attempted to force an entrance into the Babcock home. Failing to gain entrance at the door, he tried the window.

Babcock fired a shot through the window and the prowler ran back to the woods.

The Babcocks vacated the house the next day, and a party has been organized to hunt him down with dogs.[7]

————————◆————————

HE HAD A CONTEST WITH A WILD MAN

Residents of Eureka Have a Remarkable Experience in the Woods — Posse and Dogs in Pursuit.

EUREKA, CA, Jan. 18 — On Sunday last, Will Babcock, who resides on the Hayes Place, hearing an unfamiliar noise in the brush and thinking it was a bear, fired one shot into the brush.

To his intense surprise, a white man emerged from the bushes on all fours and dashed at Mrs. Babcock, who was standing

————————◆————————

A wild man of the woods is loose in the upper end of Humboldt County.[8]

————————◆————————

A wild man is wandering around in the vicinity of Eureka, and mamma and the nurse girl have only to say "bogie man" in order to get the bad little boys and girls on their good behavior.[9]

————————◆————————

Family Is Frightened by a Strange Man in the Woods

REDDING, CA, March 25 — Roaming around in the vicinity of Buckeye and the Old Diggings District is a wild man, with the proverbial long beard and flowing hair and stark naked. The women and children are afraid to go out of doors and only the other day the family of H.E. Clawson were badly frightened by the approach of the madman near their home. One of the children was playing near the house when a stone fell near him. Looking up the child saw the wild man beckoning to him and making a peculiar sound with his mouth.

The child ran into the house and informed his mother, who ran with her children to a place of safety. The wild man disappeared and it is probable that an organized effort will be made to capture him. The impression is general that the wild man is the same being that made his presence unwelcome in the vicinity of Keswick some time ago.[10]

———◆———

Redding has a regular story-book wild man running loose around its outskirts, without even the formality of a gee-string or a fig leaf in the way of wearing apparel. Some enthusiastic side-show manager should be communicated with at once.[11]

———◆———

AFTER A WILD MAN

———

PEOPLE IN SAN BERNARDINO COUNTY FEAR THE STRANGER IN THE WOODS.

———

SAN BERNARDINO, CA. May 15 — People living in the neighborhood of Devil Canyon, six miles north of this city, are greatly agitated over the appearance there of a "wild man." The fellow lives in the brush along the sides of the canyon and apparently subsists on roots and herbs. He is described as a middle aged man with long hair and only half dressed.

So far he has attempted no harm, but by his strange actions and loud screaming has badly frightened several farmers' wives living in that locality.[12]

———◆———

Huge Wild Man in Hills Near Blue Tent

MARRYSVILLE — A wild man of giant stature is roaming over the mountainous regions about Blue Tent, frightening the inhabitants of the section. He wears no clothing, but carries a gun. This probably explains why so many carcasses of bears and deer have been found lying about, each showing signs of having been more or less eat into, evidently for food. The man's resting place is thought to be a cave difficult of access and never entered by others, so far as is known, because of the great number of rattlesnakes that infest it.[13]

WILD MAN IN YUBA MOUNTAINS

MARYSVILLE, December 25. — A wild man is roaming the mountains in the neighborhood of Bullard's bar, in this county, and the residents are terrorized. Constable Owens was directed by the Sheriff over the telephone to capture the fellow, if possible, and is now off on that mission.[14]

Out Fyerstown way some "reputable citizens" have seen a wild man. The government ought to get an excise tax on some of the hard cider those people are making.[15]

WILD MAN SCARE

Both the constables of Pasadena Township have been asked to be on the lookout for an alleged wild man who has been seen in the vicinity of the Giddings Ranch, toward the mouth of Millard Canyon. According to reports, a stranger, garbed only in breechcloth and with long, flowing locks, is inhabiting the wilds of that vicinity, coming out of his haunts only rarely and, whenever seen, running swiftly to cover. Officials of the North Pasadena Water Company scout the rumor that the wild man has contaminated their water supply by bathing therein, but E.W. Giddings, owner of the Giddings Ranch, naturally does not relish a wild man about his preserves.[16]

Constable Harley Newell today made a search for a supposed wild man, who, from reports, has infested the vicinity of Devil's Gate and Giddings Ranch along the Arroyo Seco. Mr. Giddings has caught sight several times of an individual who persists in going about in nature's garb, much to the annoyance of residents and those who pass his haunts.[17]

———————◆———————

WILD MAN LOOSE

———

Escapes from Mountains to San Gabriel Valley and Ranchers Are Not Sleeping Soundly.

Ranchers in the San Gabriel Valley slept with one eye open last night ready to jump at the first squeal of a chicken. The Wild Man of San Dimas Canyon has escaped from the mountains and taken to the valley.

Whoever this individual may be who has for a week terrorized the camps in the mountains of that district, he is a man with an abnormal appetite. If he finds campers away he loots the camp of provisions, yet a short time afterward seems to be as hungry as ever.

Now that he has taken to the valley it is a question as to what his hunger will drive him to take. Constables in every township are looking for him and he will be arrested at the first opportunity. It is thought that he is insane. The man is ragged and unkempt and has three fingers missing from one hand.[18]

———————◆———————

AFTER HUMAN FREAK

Residents of Mira Mar, a residence suburb east of the city, are greatly excited about a supposed wild man roaming in that vicinity. Yesterday afternoon Mrs. Dr. W, Harriman Jones, wife of the city health officer, looking out of the rear window of her residence, saw a tattered and ragged fellow come up the road, carrying a live squirrel in each hand. He looked about stupidly, then ran into the next yard, seated himself on the grass, killed the squirrels and then devoured the raw flesh. Having gorged himself, he hid away in his rags the remainder of the animals and disappeared toward the beach. The officers are looking for the man, wondering what sort of a demon fiend he is possessed of and also where he got the live squirrels.[19]

WILD MAN

The *Pajaronian* of Saturday says that a wild man is reported to be infesting the neighborhood of Spreckels Quarry. It is believed that he sleeps in a cave nearby, from which he emerges at night for the purpose of raiding the cook house of the Matthews cattle ranch. Geo. Matthews caught him in the act the other night and sprinkled him with birdshot; but he made his escape. The man who is described as being ragged and dirty is thought to be an escaped lunatic.[20]

WILD MAN AT SEARS POINT

The people down toward Reclamation have been terrorized in the past two weeks by an alleged wild man, who is probably a lunatic — in fact he is thought to be an escapee from an asylum. He hides in the tules at day, coming out at night and subsisting on sour milk taken from the hog troughs of the near by dairies. The man is said to be six feet tall and when pursued rushes through the sloughs, ditches, and over fences. Nobody has been able to get very close to him.

The residents down that way are afraid to venture forth at night, but thus far no damage has been done to and property or harm to any person. Deputy Sheriff R.L. Rasmussen went down on Wednesday to look for the man but could not locate him.[21]

SAW THE WILD MAN

One day last week Della Maria, who conducts the Rose Ranch, saw the wild man who has been terrorizing residents of that place. The man was in the cow barn near the dairy, and when the owner of the ranch approached he made his exit. He ran over into the hills and escaped.[22]

WILD MAN AT LARGE

Deputy Sheriff Rasmussen and Constable J.B. Sullivan were summoned to the Conway Ranch near this city today to try and capture a wild man, who is at large in that locality. The man frightened the residents by his queer actions. He is a big, tall fellow, wears dark clothes and a dark hat. He is supposed to be the same one who was seen near this city last week.

Arthur Matzen and the Conway Bros. searched all day on horseback to try to find the man, but he evades them.[23]

———————◆———————

CATALINA EXCITED OVER MYSTERIOUS WILD WOMAN

———

Tourists Returning from Hunting Trips Declare They Have Seen Her Frequently, but She Eludes Pursuit

———

AVALON, Catalina Island, July 31. — A "wild woman" coming from none knows where and dwelling in what cryptic cavern of the island fastness none may guess, is the latest and most exciting sensation in Catalina.

According to boatmen and others who frequently make trips into various inlets and retreats of the magic isle, the woman is never seen before sunset, and no one has been able to get close enough to her to form any well defined conception of her appearance, except to note that she is almost nude and carries a rifle.

The "wild woman" has been seen by a number of the islanders, if their stories are to be believed, and all who claim to have seen her pronounce her exceptionally "wild" and of powerful Amazonian proportions.

Her hair, according to common report, is long and entirely unbound, flowing in spectral tresses over her bare shoulders and down to her waist. Her skin is said to be tanned, but her natural complexion, according to several who claim suddenly to have run across her in some of the canyons, is that of an Anglo-Saxon. She is described as beautiful, but timid as a fawn.

About three months ago, rumor has it, she was seen for the first time in a ravine not far from White's Landing. She appeared going over the brow of a hill, on the apex of which she paused awhile and stood gazing over the sea and leaning on her rifle.

About a month ago the "wild woman" was seen in the vicinity of the isthmus, and several boys spent nearly a day looking for her rendezvous, but without avail.

The "wild woman" completely eludes all followers, and is as nimble as a goat when it comes to running up and down hills.

At first the story of her presence on the island was discredited, but in the last few days tourists have returned to Avalon from hunting trips and verified the report. They claim to have seen her in sections of the island widely apart, indicating that she is a great traveler.

There has been some talk in Avalon of organizing a searching party to go after the woman and run her down. A number of men have volunteered, but the women here think she ought to be left alone.[24]

WILD MAN THROWS A SCARE INTO GIRL STUDENTS

STANFORD UNIVERSITY, CA, Oct. 7. — County officers are quietly looking today for a supposed maniac who attacked a party of picnickers, coeds, in the hills back of the university last Friday. Twenty pretty girls members of the Manginita Club, among whom were the two daughters of Governor Gillett, became the target for clods, earth, and sticks in the hands of the frenzied man. Two of the girls by hiding in the undergrowth succeeded in escaping. They reached the home of President

(text obscured), but it was empty. Frantic with fear for the safety of their companions they *(text obscured)*...in the darkness.[25]

SAW WILD MAN IN THE MOUNTAINS

SANTA MONICA, CA, Nov. 7 — Is there a wild man roaming the mountains of the Santa Monica range? There is, according to the story told by Bertrand Basey, who has just come down from the vicinity of point Dume, where he has been acting as commissary for the contractors engaged in the construction of the Malibu-Rindge railway.

Base says that there were frequent losses from the improvised storehouse. At first these were attributed to the thieving proclivities of coyotes and mountain squirrels but as it was found to be impossible to trap any of these animals further investigation was made, with the result of learning that the theft was due to some cunning hand whose movements were directed by a reasoning mind. He kept a strict lookout and was soon rewarded by the sight of a brown being fashioned after the form of a man, approaching the tent. The thing was on all fours, was devoid of clothing or such covering as might have been provided by the skins of animals, and had a face covered with hair.

Basey was about to fire at the intruder when he was deterred by the close resemblance of the visitor to a man. Thinking it might be a railroad laborer in disguise, he made a noise as if to frighten the thief away. Suddenly the wild thing gave forth a guttural yell, rose upright on its hind legs and disappeared in the underbrush. Nothing more was seen or heard of the mysterious half human beast, although the railroaders who went to the beach for a bath that morning are still wondering what manner of animal had been there before them to leave peculiar tracks in the sand. The tracks, which they photographed, were not unlike those that would have been left by the hands and feet of a man were he provided with long, claw-like nails for each of the five toes and the four fingers and thumb.[26]

———————◆———————

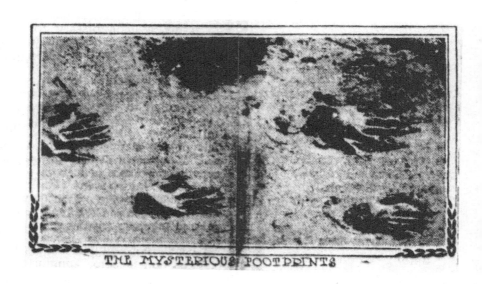

THE MYSTERIOUS FOOTPRINTS

———————◆———————

WILD MAN WORRIES OCEAN VIEW WOMEN

Police Guard Boswell's Ranch to Track Dweller in Hills North of Berkeley

BERKELEY, Dec. 30 — A wild man who frequents the neighborhood of Ocean View has eluded all efforts of the police to capture him and the women in the vicinity of Boswell's Ranch are in constant dread of being attacked.

School director James Donohue reported the case to the police, and although they have endeavored to capture the man he has made his escape in the underbrush and is still at large.

He goes barefooted and resembles a wild man in every particular, being of unkempt appearance and wearing a heavy, rough beard. He had been living in the hills farther north and only lately came to the proposed site of the capital to make his home.

Generally afraid of man, he has of late become more bold, and has frequently visited the back yards of the dwellers of the tracts north of here and frightened the women and children.

The police have positioned a guard in Boswell's Ranch to track him to his hovel. It is thought that he is insane.[27]

———————◆———————

WILD MAN LOOSE IN HILLS

Haunts Devil's Canyon and Is Giving Campers and Picnic Parties Some Bad Scares. Not an Asylum Escape.

Word reached San Bernardino last night that a wild man has been seen for the last two days in and near the head of Devil Canyon, his actions having frightened a number of persons spending an outing in that locality. The first notice of the man, so far as could be learned last night, was on Wednesday forenoon, when he startled a group of Highgrove women who had strolled away from the main group of picnickers.

Harry DeLong, a teamster, was informed of the occurrence, and meeting the individual half way down the canyon, tried to get sufficiently close to engage the man in conversation, but the stranger leaped the creek, and disappeared in the brush on the mountainside. In the afternoon the picnic party ran across the man further down the canyon, and he fled.

IDENTITY UNKNOWN

Yesterday forenoon he was met by Harry Miles and August Van Pelt, and kept well out of reach. He is described as very eccentric, and his clothes are torn into tatters from his wanderings through the brush. Inquiry at the State Hospital brought the information that no patients were missing from that institution, and it is understood that the individual who in the past has caused some alarm in that region, and is being aided in outdoor life by the Supervisors, is still in the tumble-down cabin in that quarter, and evidently recovering his health.[28]

———————◆———————

A naked hairy creature, believed to be an escaped gorilla from the Robinson Circus, which showed in Oakland last week, has been seen in Piedmont Hills. Hunting parties are seeking the creature which has frightened many people. The creature will be shot if sighted.[29]

[1] *San Francisco Call* (San Francisco, CA), March 22, 1900.

[2] *San Francisco Call* (San Francisco, CA), July 29, 1900.

[3] *The Los Angeles Times* (Los Angeles, CA), August 25, 1900.

[4] *Weekly Rogue River Courier* (Grants Pass, OR), July 4, 1901.

[5] *The Los Angeles Times* (Los Angeles, CA), July 25, 1901.

[6] *The Los Angeles Times* (Los Angeles, CA), December 29, 1901.

[7] *Oakland Tribune* (Oakland, CA), January 18, 1902.
Bigfoot creatures don't always walk upright - many reports have them dropping to all fours and running as quadrupeds. The quadrupedal locomotion of the wild man in this article points to it being a bigfoot. Likewise the fact that the creature, if that's what this was, seems to have followed the Babcocks home. Bigfoot creatures seem to have a kind of culture of revenge and, often, if shot or injured in some way, will show up at the homes of those who injured them to harass, frighten, or otherwise seek some sort of presumed revenge. Many stories have bigfoot creatures trying door handles and window latches. Whatever this was, human or bigfoot, it was scary enough to cause the Babcocks to vacate their home!

[8] *Petaluma Daily Morning Courier* (Petaluma, CA), January 20, 1902.

[9] *The Los Angeles Times* (Los Angeles, CA), January 24, 1902.

[10] *Oakland Tribune* (Oakland, CA), March 25, 1902.
Bigfoot creatures have been reported to take a special interest in human children - something I find rather disturbing. Here we have a report of stone throwing, then the being making a peculiar sound as it beckoned the child. Human or bigfoot, this is a disturbing report.

[11] *The Los Angeles Times* (Los Angeles, CA), March 28, 1902.

[12] *Oakland Tribune* (Oakland, CA), May 15, 1902.

[13] *Daily Review* (Hayward, CA), September 26, 1902.

[14] *San Francisco Chronicle* (San Francisco, CA), December 26, 1902.

[15] *The San Bernardino County Sun* (San Bernardino, CA), January 1, 1904.

[16] *The Los Angeles Times* (Los Angeles, CA), June 3, 1905.

[17] *Los Angeles Herald* (Los Angeles, CA), June 3, 1905.
    It is interesting to note that the same incident, reported on the same day, by two different papers has one notable difference: one paper has the "wild man" clothed in a breechcloth - the other in "nature's garb" i.e. naked. This further convinces me that I may be right in my suspicions that some reporters or newspaper editors added clothing to the wild man reports, for whatever reasons.
    Also note here, and elsewhere in this volume, the frequent occurrence of place names with "Devil" in the title: Devil's Gate, Devil's Canyon, Devil's Hole, etc. Bigfoot researchers in the past have noted how frequently creature sightings occur in and around these "Devil"-named locales.

[18] *The Los Angeles Times* (Los Angeles, CA), August 5, 1906.

[19] *The Los Angeles Times* (Los Angeles, CA), August 19, 1906.
    This story almost certainly concerns a human, but I hope the reader will forgive my decision to include it here. It's just so weird and wonderful that I could not resist. Where *did* he get those squirrels?!?

[20] *Santa Cruz Weekly Sentinel* (Santa Cruz, CA), October 20, 1906.

[21] *Petaluma Argus-Courier* (Petaluma, CA), May 21, 1908.

[22] *Petaluma Daily Morning Courier* (Petaluma, CA), June 1, 1908.

[23] *Petaluma Daily Morning Courier* (Petaluma, CA), July 31, 1908.

[24] *Los Angeles Herald* (Los Angeles, CA), August 1, 1908.

[25] *Medford Mail Tribune* (Medford, OR), October 7, 1908.
    The text of this article was unfortunately obscured - I have printed as much as I could decipher here.

[26] *The Spokane Press* (Spokane, WA), November 9, 1908.

[27] *The San Francisco Call* (San Francisco, CA), December 31, 1908

[28] *The San Bernardino County Sun* (San Bernardino, CA), April 30, 1909.

[29] *Oakland Tribune* (Oakland, CA), September 29, 1909.

V. HE IN EVERY WAY RESEMBLED A LARGE APE

CALIFORNIA 1910 - 1922

WILD MAN FADES INTO THIN AIR

Fearsome Apparition Dispelled by Posse of Deputies from Sheriff's Office.

A raging wild man with a mouth aflame, gloating eyes and clad in an upholstery of waving hair, who has tormented the minds and inspired the fears of those of the Claremont district, was routed this morning by a posse under command of Deputy Sheriff Sweeney. The fearful nightmare that has wracked the fearsome minds of the Berkeleys turned out to be a simple lover of wild nature who abides in the old Fish Ranch Road Canyon. He gives his name as Jack Hallowell, his occupation as gardener, his age as 45, and he is a bachelor.

Hallowell lives in a dugout on a deep ravine far from the "maddening crowd" and about three or four hundred yards northeasterly from the Claremont Hotel.

The recluse laughs at the assertion that he is the fearful apparition that has befrighted the vicinity of Claremont.[1]

---◆---

"WILD MAN" INVADES FORT JONES DISTRICT

Seen by Women and is Believed to Be Indian

GREENVIEW, May 3. — Residents of the vicinity of Fort Jones are in the midst of a wild man scare. Several women in that neighborhood have seen the man, but he has not yet been captured. It is believed he is an Indian. He looks the part of a wild man, with long hair and a scarred face.[2]

WILD MAN SCARES WOMAN
THOUGHT TO BE CRAZY LEPER.

YREKA, May 3. — An unknown wild man, half nude, has caused terror near Indian Creek, about eight miles from Fort Jones, this county. He has been seen by several women in the past few days, and they have been greatly frightened. Their stories have caused much alarm. Women who have seen the wild man describe him as having a savage look and acting more like an animal than a human being. Some who have had a nearer view of him say he is suffering from some horrible disease, probably leprosy. He is a white man. A request was sent here from the county authorities to capture the man, and the deputy sheriffs will attempt to do so.[3]

It is said there is a wild man living somewhere on Kern River between the Kern Island Canal and the Canyon. A party under leadership of Zip Coons has been organized to capture him alive.[4]

Covina has a "wild man" who has been stealing eggs of the ranchers. With eggs at 50 cents a dozen, he may be wild all right, but he is not crazy.[5]

Thinks Wild Men Infest Hills

REDWOOD CITY, May 29. — From the discovery of a body on the Visitacion Hills and developments in the case, there has come the firm belief in the minds of authorities of San Mateo County that the evident murder is one of several and that the disappearance of several travelers might be traced to the machinations of a gang of half-demented creatures, posing as wild men, infesting the fastness of the mountain range. Basing their theories on the statements of Juan Goivl, one of the alleged wild men, who two months ago was arrested and incarcerated on a charge of vagrancy, the sheriff is making a sweeping investigation.

The original belief that there was but one wild man of the hills and that the murder mystery could be cleared up by him was shattered by the declaration of A.F. Morris, proprietor of the Guadalupe Dairy, which is situated half a mile from the hidden grave where the body was found. From him it was learned that the hills were infested by a regular gang of hermits, men of unkempt appearance and ferocious aspect, who prowled around the railroad tracks at all hours of the day and whose livings were obtained in a manner emphatically mysterious.

6

◆

WILD MAN ALARMS CAMPERS

Sojourners at Oakglen in
San Bernardino Mountains
See Hairy Creature
Who Is Fleet of Foot.

REDLANDS, Sept. 17. — Consternation reigns among the women folks and some of the men in the wilds around Oakglen, caused by the appearance of a supposedly crazy man during the past week. The man, who has been described as unkempt, with long hair, has been seen several times and his actions are such as to cause considerable uneasiness among those sojourning at the summer resort.

People who came down from the canyon this morning confirmed the report. It is said that the man made his appearance about a week ago. He first made his appearance at night, by creeping up to the different cottages, and he was evidently searching for food. When an attempt was made to capture him he fled with the speed of a deer and would remain in hiding, only making his appearance again when forced to by hunger.

Some two weeks ago a man with a long black beard,

dressed in a very shabby fashion, was seen at the mouth of Green Canyon, leading into Mill Creek Canyon, about ten miles from Oakglen, where he has been seen lately.

The queer character has, on several occasions, crept cautiously up behind women and stood there, making no attempt, however, at doing harm, but succeeding in causing the women to run and scream.

It is believed that the man is an escaped patient from Patton. Local officers have been notified.[7]

————————◆————————

WILD MAN ANNOYS OAK GLEN FOLKS

———

Long Hair and Few Clothes, and He Hangs Around For Campers' Scraps.

———

Redlands *Review*: Reports from Oak Glen are to the effect that a wild man or perhaps a crazy man, or maybe a little of bit of both, is lurking in the jungles and wilds in that vicinity and naturally the women folks are afraid to go out to the well to get a pail of water now. It seems that the only real trouble with the man is that he is always hungry.

It is said that the man made his first appearance about a week ago. He is described as having a long matted beard, long hair, and generally wild appearance — and few clothes. Some of the most daring even suggest that he is dressed only in what nature allows him and not according to the provisions and letter of the law.

It seems that the fellow has not offered violence to anyone but has been seen eating banana peels and other trash left by campers. There is a theory that he is an escaped lunatic from Patton.[8]

————————◆————————

What a white man will do or will not do is one of the things that is not only beyond finding out but is without the pale of guesswork. The dispatches yesterday tell of the sheriff and ten deputy sheriffs armed with guns and carrying ropes, searching the wilds around Devil's Canyon in San Bernardino, California, for "a naked wild man with long hair and whiskers," who has terrorized the campers in that satanic section. Down in southern Oregon a gang of spectacled wiseacres are camping in the woods waiting for a naked man to get through doing the Nebuchadnezzar stunt and to come out of the pristine forest covered with bark, furs, or anything else he can find to hide under. The one is pronounced crazy and the other an artist and hero. Maybe it's the whiskers that make the difference, and the long hair the distinction.[9]

———————◆———————

There is a wild man reported in the vicinity of Stockton. Maybe somebody handed him a counterfeit dollar.[10]

———————◆———————

Search Is On for New "Wild Man" in California Desert

CHICO, CA, March 6 — Another Ishi, aboriginal inhabitant of the North American continent, has been located in the wilds of Deer Creek, according to George Bushwell of Chico, who returned here today from a trip in the wild country. He declares he found the tracks of the aborigine two miles from the place where Ishi, the child of nature who startles scientists of the University of California, was found.

Bushwell declared he is convinced that another "wild man," similar in habits to Ishi, now inhabits the almost impregnable fastness along Deer Creek. His tracks were found in the soft red dirt of that region and they are so large as to indicate a man of immense size, Bushwell said. Searching parties started out today from Chico in an effort to locate the "wild man."[11]

———————◆———————

A wild man is reported roaming at liberty in San Francisquito Canyon. Nothing especially exciting about that. With the reign of the "drys" there are any number of wild men.[12]

———————◆———————

BURGLAR LOOKS LIKE HUGE APE

———

LOS ANGELES, June 5. — The shaggy orang-outang in Poe's Murders in the Rue Morgue could have been no more horrifying in appearance than the man or beast who, at 3 o'clock on a recent morning, invaded the bedroom of two small girls in Long Beach.

The tiny daughters of H.H. Thompson were asleep in

their room in the Thompson home at 3109 Corto Place, when they were awakened by a man in the room. They screamed and huddled under the bedclothes in fear.

Thompson, the father, heard the screams and rushed into the room just in time to see the most gorilla-like man he had ever seen climbing out of the window. Before the girls' father could reach the window the man had dropped to the ground and escaped.

Thompson says the man's head and face were so covered with long, black, shaggy hair that, with his immense size and ferocious stoop, he in every way resembled a large ape. The father arrived before anything had been stolen.

The Long Beach police are hunting for a man of this ape-like description, but so far without success.[13]

sheepherders that a nude "wild man" had been seen running at large in that section.

Felix Fagoa, prominent herd owner of that district, who brought in the first report Thursday, said that a wild figure had been seen through field glasses galloping madly over the hills.

Constable R.C. Thompson of Alpaugh, who was notified, immediately organized a party, and together with A. Ellis and F.K. Ray, conducted a 24-hour search for their man. The party, which was armed with guns and ropes, claimed to have seen the man late Thursday evening, but that he escaped owing to the darkness. The search was abandoned by the constable yesterday afternoon, but sheepherders are still searching for the man in the desolate country six miles east of Alpaugh.[14]

———————◆———————

Nude "Wild Man" Seen Galloping on Hills Stirs Scare In Fresno County

———

FRESNO, March 19. — Excitement ran high at Alpaugh, southwest of here, yesterday, following the report by frightened

———————◆———————

POSSE TO HUNT COUNTRYSIDE FOR "WILD MAN"

———

YREKA, Sept. 26. — Working under the direction of Sheriff Calkins, a posse yesterday searched the countryside south of here for a scantily-clad man who is believed to be demented and who has been seen roaming the highways and darting in and out of the thickets for the last two weeks.

The posse will resume the hunt today, the sheriff said. The man sought is said to be harmless and is reported to be able to run with the fleetness of a deer. Yesterday a deputy sheriff and some tourists tried to catch the fellow, but he outran them and disappeared. He is said to have been dressed in a shirt and breachclout. It is thought he has a secret camping place in the timber.[15]

———————◆———————

[1] *Oakland Tribune* (Oakland, CA), March 10, 1910.

Another example of the "any solution will do" style of debunking given by newspapers and police. It sounds like what was being reported was something very much like a bigfoot. The police found a human living the 1910-equivalent of "off grid" and proclaimed 'we found him' and the newspapers duly reported 'they found him'. Never mind that what the people reported seeing was very different.

[2] *The San Francisco Call* (San Francisco, CA), May 4, 1910.

[3] *The Los Angeles Times* (Los Angeles, CA), May 4, 1910.

[4] *The Bakersfield Californian* (Bakersfield, CA), September 17, 1910.

[5] *The Los Angeles Times* (Los Angeles, CA), December 1, 1910.

[6] *Modesto News* (Modesto, CA), May 29, 1911.

A murder. Missing people. Gangs of wild men of "ferocious aspect". It may not be a group of bigfoot, but there is enough strangeness here to question just what these "wild men" were.

[7] *The Los Angeles Times* (Los Angeles, CA), September 18, 1912.

[8] *The San Bernardino County Sun* (San Bernardino, CA), September 19, 1912.

This and the above article present another example of conflicting reports about the wild man's dress. The "daring" suggest he may be naked. He was either naked or not - it is a window in to times past to think it was "daring" to even report a naked man or creature as the case may be.

[9] *Daily Capital Journal* (Salem, OR), July 22, 1914.

[10] *The Los Angeles Times* (Los Angeles, CA), January 24, 1916.

[11] *The Seattle Star* (Seattle, WA), March 6, 1918.

Ishi, named in this article, was a "wild man" of a different sort. The last known member of the First Nations Yahi tribe, Ishi was, at the time, declared the "last wild Indian" in America. At age 50, Ishi walked out of the California wilderness and into the white/European culture of 20th Century California towns. Hunger and a series of forest fires had driven Ishi out of the wilds. "Ishi" is an adopted name - it means "man" in the Yahi language. Tradition among the Yahi dictated that a person could not name himself until formally introduced by another Yahi. As there were no Yahi left to introduce him, he could not speak his own name. As such, he was given the alternate name of Ishi by an anthropologist. Ishi's incredibly sad and powerful life story has been told in several other books and at least one film if the reader is interested, and while he is *very interesting,* Ishi isn't the sort of wild-man we are concerned with in this volume.

The footprints mentioned in this article do concern us, however, considering the size. They certainly sound like bigfoot tracks.

[12] *The Los Angeles Times* (Los Angeles, CA), May 16, 1920.

[13] *Oakland Tribune* (Oakland, CA), June 5, 1920.

A terrifying encounter, be it man or beast that crawled through the window. Note that the father, not the children, describe the immense and ape-like look of the home invader which, to my mind, lends credibility to the story.

[14] *San Francisco Chronicle* (San Francisco, CA), March 20, 1921.

[15] *Oakland Tribune* (Oakland, CA), September 26, 1922.

VI. NATURAL CURIOSITIES

OREGON 1857 - 1887

FORKS OF WILLAMETTE, LANE COUNTY, MAY 25, 1857

Dear Sir — A most wonderful and thrilling adventure has recently occurred in the southern part of this county. A few weeks since, it appears, a man and a boy started in a quest of some lost cattle, and they had traveled a considerable distance from home when night overtook them far away from any human habitation, and building a fire, they lay down to sleep beneath the spreading branches of a stately fir tree. Towards midnight the boy was awakened by a loud plaintive cry that appeared to emanate from a human being in distress not far distant from the spot where he reclined. Springing to his feet with alacrity, and without disturbing his companion, he approached the spot from whence proceeded this, to him, singularly forlorn outcry; he had not advanced many steps however, when he observed an object approaching him that appeared like a man about twelve or fifteen feet high, of athletic proportions, with glaring eyes which had the appearance of liquid balls of fire. The monster drew near to the boy who was unable, from fright, to move a single step, and seizing him by the arm, dragged him forcibly away towards the mountains, over logs, underbrush, swamps, rivers and land with a velocity that seemed to our hero like flying. They had traveled in this manner perhaps an hour and a quarter, when the monster sunk upon the earth apparently exhausted. Our hero then became aware that this creature was indeed a *wild man*, whose body was completely covered with shaggy brown hair, about four inches in length; some of his teeth protruded from his mouth like tusks, his hands were armed with formidable claws instead of fingers, but his feet, singular to relate, appeared natural, being clothed with moccasins similar to those worn by Indians. Our hero had scarcely made these observations when the "wild man" suddenly started onward as before, never for a moment relaxing his grip on the boy's arm, which had now become painful indeed. They had not proceeded far before they entered an almost impenetrable thicket of logs and undergrowth, when the "wild man" stopped, reclined upon a log, and gave one shriek, terrific and prolonged, the reverberations of which seemed to continue for the space of five minutes; immediately after which the earth opened at their feet, as if a trap door, ingeniously contrived, had just been raised. Entering at once this subterranean abode by a ladder rudely constructed of hazel brush, they proceeded downward,

perhaps 150 or 200 feet, when they reached the bottom of a vast cave, which was brilliantly illuminated with a peculiar phosphorescent light, and water trickled from the sides of the cave in minute jets, the appearance of which was indeed singular. Above, the cave seemed slightly arched, the ceiling apparently composed of seashells of every conceivable shape and color; the bottom was, or appeared to be thickly strewn with the bones of many kinds of animals, the sight of which impressed our hero with a fearful presentiment of his own impending fate. As our hero thus closely observed the interior of this awful cave, the "wild man" left him, as if instinctively called away before partaking of his midnight repast of "roasted boy." Presently the huge monster returned by a side door, leading gently by the hand a young and delicate female of almost miraculous grace and beauty, who had doubtless been immured in this dreadful dungeon for years. As they approached our hero, the young lady fell upon her knees, and in some unknown language, in plaintive accents seemed to plead for the privilege of remaining forever in the cave of the "wild man." This singular conduct caused our hero to imagine that the "wild man," conscience stricken, had resolved to set at liberty his lovely victim, by placing her in charge of our hero, whom he had evidently captured for that purpose. As this thought passed through the mind of our hero, his ears were greeted with the strains of the most unearthly music which came from the innermost recesses of the cave. The "wild man" wept piteously as he listened to the sweet voice of the charmer, commingled with the wild music, and sobbing like a child, his handkerchief moist with grief, he raised her very carefully from her recumbent posture, and led her gently away as they had come. A moment afterwards, the damsel returned alone and advancing towards our hero with ladylike modesty and grace, placed in his hands a beautifully embossed card, upon which appeared the following words, traced in the most exquisite hand evidently the lady's own, "Boy, depart hence forthwith, or remain and be devoured." Our hero looked up, but the lady had vanished. However, he acted at once upon the hint implied by these words, and commenced retracing his steps towards the "ladder of hazel brush" which he shortly reached and commenced the ascent. Upon arriving at the top, his horror may be imagined when he found the aperture closed. The cold sweat stood on his brow, his frame quivered with mental

agony, when, after a moment, he bethought himself of a small barlow knife (a present from a near relative), he carried in his pocket, with which he instantly commenced picking the earth, being careful not to cut too near the spot where the ladder was made fast, for fear of precipitating himself to the bottom of the cave. After laboring in this manner a short time, he was rejoiced to see daylight through the earth, and he was not much longer in working a hole large enough through which he was enabled to crawl; then, having refreshed himself at a clear running brook close by, he wandered he knew not whither; it was midday when he made his escape from the cave, and he traveled that day and night, and the following day until about half past four o'clock PM, when he encountered a small party of miners prospecting for gold on the headwaters of South Umpqua River, to whom he told the story of his adventure; they listened in silence, evidently disbelieving every word, but as they could not otherwise account for the presence of our hero in that desolate region, they all said nothing, but gave him to eat and to drink.

Our hero reached the house of his father in due time; he related his adventure — the neighbors called in — he told the same story; the circuit preacher called — the story was the same; at first they smiled, then doubted, then believed: and the whole neighborhood are now prepared to make affidavit to the principal facts.

The boy is a mild, modest, moral boy, about thirteen years of age, of fair complexion, and has always borne a character for truthfulness. His parents are moral and religious people, and it is hoped that out of respect to their feelings, the story will not be disbelieved as a general thing, although many parts of it are truly wonderful.[1]

———————◆———————

A wild man is causing a sensation in the vicinity of Portland, Oregon, and the Sheriff with a large posse is out in search of him.[2]

———————◆———————

A wild woman was chasing the children at Beaver Creek schoolhouse on Wednesday, says the Oregon City *Courier*. Her long hair is disheveled and a few rags cover her nakedness. The children relate that they have seen her lying down by a log asleep.

Several men went out immediately to hunt for her in the woods but could find no trace of her whereabouts. No human being of the feminine gender is missed from the neighborhood, and where she comes from is a mystery.[3]

———————◆———————

Veritable Wild Man in the Mountains

PORTLAND, December 26th. — Much excitement has been created in the neighborhood of Lebanon recently over the discovery of a wild man in the mountains above that place, who is supposed to be the long lost John Mackentire. About four years ago Mackentire, of Lebanon, while out hunting in the mountains east of Albany with another man, mysteriously disappeared, and no definite trace of him has ever since been found. A few days ago Mr. Fitzgerald and others, while hunting in the vicinity of the butte known as Bald Peter, situated in the Cascades, several miles above any settlement, saw a man resembling the long-lost man, entirely destitute of clothing, who had grown as hairy as an animal, and was a complete wild man. He was eating the raw flesh of a deer when he was first seen, and they approached within a few yards before he saw them and fled. Isaac Banty saw this man in the same locality about two years ago. It is believed by many that the unfortunate man who was lost became deranged and managed to find means of subsistence while wandering about in the mountains, probably finding shelter in some cave. A party of several men is being organized to go in search of the man.[4]

———————◆———————

The report of a wild man being seen in the mountains and supposed to be J. McEntire, that has been published in two or three papers, is considered a purely sensational article. There have been hunters from here around Bald Peter that scoff at the idea of a human being being able to live there. As far as Mr. Banty is concerned, he never seemed to impress anyone that it was a fact, and no one thought he placed much reliance on it himself. People generally thought it was a dream or a vision produced by an overdose of salmon berries or from climbing the dizzying heights of Bald Peter. Please give Scio the

credit of the discovery, as none of our hunters know anything about it.[5]

———————◆———————

Natural Curiosities

The Ninety-seven-year-old man who cracks nuts with his teeth and chops wood Saturdays is slow in showing up this season. He was due in Douglas County on the 1st. The wild woman is on time. She has been heard from near Philomath. It is alleged that she "was seen at Wood schoolhouse, in Blodgett's Valley, June 29th, picking up crumbs where children had eaten dinner, and on the 30th she attempted to seize a little girl about twenty feet from the schoolhouse. The teacher being called, ran to the window to get, if possible, a view of her face, but did not succeed, for she bounded away like a wild animal." The Eastern Oregon hermit in a cave is due August 1st and about the 15th prox. we ought to be hearing of the chickens in Prineville that had 87 cents worth of gold in their crops when they were killed. The sea serpent seems to be as hopelessly missing this year as the July salmon.[6]

[1] *Weekly Oregon Statesman* (Salem, OR), June 9, 1857.
    A wondrous story that gets very very strange. I knew enough of faerie lore to know this sounded a lot like those tales, and so I turned the commentary for this article over to friend and fellow author. Joshua Cutchin, who has explored faerie lore more deeply than I. Joshua's commentary:

    What appears at first blush to be a Bigfoot encounter reveals a peculiar resonance with European faerie beliefs. In Celtic lore, faeries preferred abducting male children "of fair complexion," sometimes luring them into the wilderness with strange cries; even more explicitly, the descent of the "wild man" into a subterranean "trap door" is reminiscent of *souterrains*, underground dwellings historically found in faerie forts throughout the British Isles. This underground space, with its peculiar indirect illumination, resembles traditional descriptions of Faerie Land – as well as, it may be noted, spaces perceived in psychedelic experiences (the similarities between faerie lore and altered states of consciousness are striking; in this case, the arched, colorful, decorated ceiling is a recurring feature of those who have used DMT, the beauty of which parallels Faerie Land). While in this space, the witness allegedly hears "the most unearthly music," another hallmark of faerie lore. Perhaps the most affronting connection between this yarn and European folklore can be found in the wild man's captive: it was not uncommon for those trapped among faeries to encounter fellow mortals, who passed on advice about how to avoid further imprisonment. Finally, the use of a knife in the boy's escape finds antecedent in a Scottish legend, wherein a father keeps the door open to Faerie Land by thrusting his dirk into its threshold.

    Check out Joshua's books *The Brimstone Deceit* and *A Trojan Feast* (both published by Anomalist Books) and find more at www.JoshuaCutchin.com.

[2] *Petaluma Weekly Argus* (Petaluma, CA), June 30, 1883.

[3] *Corvallis Gazette-Times* (Corvallis, OR), June 20, 1884.

[4] *The Record-Union* (Sacramento, CA), December 28, 1885.
    Here we have an example of the idea, somewhat prevalent at the time, that a man could grow hair all over his body should he reject civilization or become lost in the wilderness. Of course, this simply does not happen in humans - genetics precludes this possibility.

[5] *Albany Democrat* (Albany, OR), January 1, 1886.
And here we have an example of a rival paper "debunking" the rumors. This "logic" is often used to this day: "I'm a hunter and I've never seen anything like that, so it doesn't exist" - an argument that holds no water. That said, they are in disbelief that a *human* could survive in those mountains and I am asserting that it isn't a human about which the above article was reporting, but a bigfoot creature.

[6] *San Francisco Chronicle* (San Francisco, CA), July 18, 1887.

VII. OF GIANT STATURE

OREGON 1891 - 1897

Wild men are next to sea serpents in the list of curiosities. The *Ashland Record* is trying to work up a boom as follows: A wild man has been seen several times of late in the vicinity of John Obenchain's, near Big Butte, Jackson County. He is naked and takes to the woods every time he sights a human being. The nearest he was seen to the haunts of a human being was at a country school house, where it was supposed he was prowling around for some waste lunches left by the school children.[1]

Another Wild Man.

A sheepherder brought in the report Monday from the John Day that a veritable "wild man of the woods" had been seen near sheep camps in that section. Several people have run across him, it is said, but as is customary with wild men he has always disappeared at their approach. The reported presence of the creature has caused much excitement up there, and an organized attempt may be made to capture him, which should be encouraged by the Robinson's Circus management.[2]

Running Wild in the Woods.

———

For some time rumors have reached us, says the Vale, Malheur County, *Gazette*, about a wild man ranging between Beulah and the Harper ranch, but not until within the last few days have the reports gained currency.

How and whence the stranger came no one seems to know. Ranch hands have heard strange noises among the willows, or the wild wail of a human blended with the lonesome yelps of coyotes.

Last Thursday the doubtful clouds were dissipated from the minds of the skeptical. Among the other hands that went to work Thursday morning on the Harper ranch was Floyd Garrison, with a team of mules, who started to mow the lower field. He had not been gone long when he was seen coming toward the house at a breakneck speed, and, with team foaming and face as white as chalk, proceeded to tell his story.

He had not gone but a round or two when he was aroused by a series of incoherent yells, and out of the brush came the form of a man, with scanty a rag about his loins, eyes wild and protruding from their sockets, and his emaciated body was covered with short hair of a dark color.

On seeing Garrison he turned, and, with an agonizing scream, fled through the brush.

As yet, no steps have been taken to capture him.[3]

———◆———

Wild Man of the John Day Precinct

———

ASTORIA, OR, Sept. 21 — The residents of John Day precinct, in this county, report that an insane man has been seen in the woods there, running about in an almost nude state. He is described as being six feet tall, with long black hair and whiskers. He will allow no one to approach him, and, when surprised, seeks cover in the brush. How he subsists is a mystery, as none of the settlers has any idea where he obtains food.[4]

———◆———

A trapper who has been hunting and trapping on the Malheur River south of the agency valley this winter, reports to the *Vale Advocate* one of those prodigies of nature known as a wild man. The *Advocate* says the biped is of giant stature, being at

76

least seven feet high, having long and massive arms that reach to its knees, while the whole body is covered with curly, glossy hair.[5]

————————◆————————

[1] *Albany Democrat* (Albany, OR) May 29, 1891.

[2] *Albany Democrat* (Albany, OR) July 29, 1892.

[3] *The Medford Mail* (Medford, OR) August 24, 1894.

[4] *St. Helens Mist* (St. Helens, OR) September 25, 1896.

[5] *Lincoln County Leader* (Toledo, OR) April 8, 1897.

VIII. THE HORROR OF THE MINERS

OREGON 1900 - 1908

YOUNG MAN KILLED BY CRAZY LOGGER

Was Assisting Officers to Arrest the Man When He Was Laid Low by a Rifle Ball.

ASTORIA, OR, Jan. 19 — Lake Moore, a young logger living about ten miles south of this city, was killed about 4:30 this afternoon while aiding the county authorities in an effort to apprehend Mat Hilstrom, a crazy logger. The demented man labored under the hallucination that the woods were full of gorillas, and three times this week attempted to kill L.R. Abercrombe, a neighbor. Twice Mrs. Hilstrom quieted her crazy spouse, but this morning he watched for Abercrombie on a road and took a shot at him. The bullet did not miss Abercrombie's head by more than an inch. Abercrombie then came to the city and acquainted the county authorities with the situation.

Deputy Sheriff Trullinger and Constable Wickman left for the house. On the way out they met young Moore, who agreed to accompany them and point out Hilstrom's abode.

When they reached the place Moore suggested it would be better that he should go to the door, as he was acquainted with the crazy man.

Mrs. Hilstrom appeared in response to the knock at the door. Moore asked where Hilstrom was and he had no sooner uttered the words than the report of a rifle rang out. Moore staggered backward with a groan and fell dead. The body lay only a few feet from the door and the officers deemed it folly to attempt to recover it, as Hilstrom would doubtlessly shoot them when they appeared in sight. Constable Wickman remained at the place while Deputy Trillinger hurried in the launch to the city. A posse left at once for the scene and the house is now surrounded. Further bloodshed is feared when the effort to get him from the house is made.[1]

◆

A WILD MAN IN POLK COUNTY

DALLAS, May 23. — A party searching for the wild man near Falls City reported having seen him. The party consisted of about 20 men, and it will be augmented 100, from all parts of the county.

There is no doubt but that there is a man who runs away when seen, and who is of a wild appearance. At least 10 responsible men have seen him and all give the same description. 20 men left Dallas yesterday morning to assist in the capture if possible.

A.R. Handy, who is supposed by many to be this wild man, disappeared on December 30, 1898.[2]

◆

THE WILD MAN OF POLK COUNTY

CORNALLIS, May 25. — Joseph H. Wilson, of this city, has left for Falls City, to engage there in the search for the wild man. Mr. Wilson is a son-in-law of A.K. Handy, who disappeared 17 months ago. Mr. Wilson has been in constant communication with the searching parties, and has information that has made him much interested in the search. The wild man is, Mr. Wilson says, about the size of his missing father-in-law.

On three different days the stranger has been seen, and in all by several persons, once at a distance of 15 feet. He was spoken to, and in reply gave vent to a gurgling sound and then ran away. Each time he ran up the creek, twice going north and once west. A camp of several men has been established by the sheriff in the vicinity, for the purpose of keeping a watch. Mr. Wilson expects to remain there until the mystery shall be solved.

There is much interest here in the case. Mr. Handy resided here several years, and had a wide circle of friends. When he disappeared he was 48 years of age, and still a strong man. Nearly all his life he had lived in a cold country and was accustomed to life in the snow. This knowledge has a tendency to encourage those acquainted with the facts to believe that when Handy disappeared, December 30, 1898, he might have weathered the severe snow storm that prevailed then and afterwards, escaping only with the delirium that seems to be characteristic of the erratic stranger in the vicinity of Falls City.[3]

———————◆———————

The boogy man has been seen over in Eastern Oregon. They call it "the kangaroo man." They say the creature has the shape of a man, but is of enormous size and covered with hair. He is supposed to eat miners raw without any salt, and has been seen to jump from one mountain peak to another, all the while emitting blood-curdling yells and spouting sulphurous flames from his nostrils. What kind of whiskey do they sell over in that country anyway?[4]

———————◆———————

A wild man is said to invest the woods near the Pop Corn school house — at times.[5]

———————◆———————

We are informed that a determined effort is being made to capture the "Kangaroo Man" who is supposed to be roaming in the wilds of the Sixes River country, terrorizing the tenderfoot prospectors in that region and destroying the game supply to satisfy his insatiable desire for spilling blood, tells the Cos Bay News. An Eastern man, who has handled freaks in the show business for a number of years, was in town last week, and gained much information from Levi and Al Smith regarding the wild man; his habits, his appetite for lone prospectors, and the probable location of the cave which he makes his winter quarters. A hunting party is to be organized in the near future and should they succeed in capturing him he will be exhibited in the principal cities of the United States and European countries.[6]

———————◆———————

Coos Bay News: Stories of the Sixes River wild man are coming in early this year. The Myrtle Point *Enterprise* learns that the Kangaroo Man was seen three times since the 10th of last month. Two men, Ward and Burlison, saw the monster plainly, and took a shot at him, but failed to bag him. At last accounts he was still roaming the wilds of the mining region, ready to gobble up tenderfoot prospectors, whom, it is presumed, he eats without salt.[7]

A GIGANTIC WILD MAN TERRORIZES RANCHERS AND MINERS IN OREGON

Is Said to Be Seven Feet tall and Strong as an Ox

Has Been Shot at Several Times Which May Be What Has Made Him Mad

ROSEBURG, OR, March 25. — A wild man is reported to be loose in the mountains of Coos County. He is described as seven feet tall, muscular and unkempt. He has been terrorizing ranchers and miners until they are discussing the project of an organized hunt.

The man has been shot twice without effect. He is believed to be an insane prospector of gigantic stature.[8]

COOS COUNTY HAS GIGANTIC WILD MAN

ROSEBURG, OR, March 25. — It is reported here that a wild man has been seen by several Coos County miners in the backwoods district. He is described as being nearly seven feet tall, with large arms and legs. Three times since February 10 he has disturbed the cabins in which miners were sleeping by shaking them. Twice he was fired at, with no visible effect except to cause him to retreat. Many of the settlers near the place of his appearance are in abject fear of the creature and are almost ready to leave the vicinity.

What lends authenticity to the story is the fact that in years past persons have reported seeing at different times such a man. Those residing in the district are discussing a systematic attempt for his capture.[9]

THE SIXES WILD MAN AGAIN

Hairy Being Who Is Horror of the Miners

He Hurls Four Pound Rocks Through the Air Like Baseballs

The Appearance again of the "wild man" of the Sixes has thrown some of the miners into a state of excitement and fear. A report says the wild man has been seen three times since the 10th of last month. The first appearance occurred on "Thompson Flat." Wm. Ward and a young man by the name of Burlison were sitting by the fire in their cabin one night when they heard something walking around the cabin which resembled a man walking and when it came to the corner of the cabin it took hold of the corner and gave the building a vigorous shake and kept up a frightful noise all the time — the same that has so many times warned the venturesome miners of the approach of the hairy man and caused them to flee in abject fear. Mr. Ward walked to the cabin door and could see the monster plainly as it walked away and took a shot at it with his rifle, but the bullet went wild of its mark.

The last appearance of the animal was at the Harrison cabin only a few days ago. Mr. Ward was at the Harrison cabin this time and again figured in the excitement. About 5 o'clock in the morning the wild man gave the door of the cabin a vigorous shaking, which aroused Ward and one of the Harrison boys who took their guns and started in to do the disturber. Ward fired at the man and he answered by sending a four-pound rock at Ward's head, but his aim was a little too high. He then disappeared in the brush.

Many of the miners avow that the wild man is a reality. They have seen him and know whereof they speak. They say he is something after the fashion of a gorilla and unlike anything else either in appearance or action. He can outrun or jump anything else that has ever been known; and not only that but he can throw rocks with wonderful force and accuracy. He is about seven feet high, has broad hands and feet and his body is covered by a prolific growth of hair. In short he looks like the very devil.[10]

———————◆———————

WALLOWA LAKE MOST BEAUTIFUL

STRANGE INDIAN LEGENDS CONCERNING IT

Growing in Popularity as a Summer Resort — Will Be Converted Into a Magnificent Resort on Completion of Wallowa Branch of O.R.& N. — Rarely Ever Freezes Over Until in January or February.

The famous Wallowa Lake, one mile south of this place, is now a sheet of ice, and the satisfaction of skaters is supreme, says a dispatch from Joseph. While smaller lakes usually freeze over in December, this lake rarely cools sufficiently to freeze until February.

Wallowa Lake is five miles long and about one mile wide, and in the center is about 280 feet deep. Its elevation is 4550 feet above sea level and is about 150 feet above the elevation of Joseph.

The beauty of Wallowa Lake is a theme worthy of the brush of any artist. Its surface is usually without a ripple, and the deep blue of its waters, the gray slope of the ridges on either side, with their sharp outlines above, the dark green forests on the mountainsides, and, finally the mountain peaks in fantastic robes of snow, form a natural scene rarely equaled.

At present the chief use the lake is put to is a summer resort, though it forms a natural reservoir for an immense supply of water, which, with the development of the upper Wallowa Valley, sure to follow the completion of the Joseph - Elgin branch of the O. R. & N. company, is certain to be required for irrigating purposes. Several ditches now tap the Wallowa River, its outlet, but only a very small part of the possibilities of the lake is utilized.

Many Indian legends and superstitions cluster about the lake. The name is of Indian origin, being pronounced as the word allow is. By some, it is urged Wallowa means "fish-trap" in the Indian tongue. Others say the Indians who always fished in the lake would leave their fish traps in the lake during the winter months, weighing them down with upright poles, to which rocks were fastened at the bottom, and cross pieces at the top, to designate the location. Since the Indians spoke of the lake as Wallowa, it is contended that they had in mind these crosses, and, therefore, Wallowa means cross.

The Indians never would venture near the middle of the lake. As a legend runs, an Indian brave long ago encountered a strange monster in the solitude of the mountains, which he followed to the lake's edge, then into the quiet stillness of its surface, and on to the middle, where, after a brief struggle, the monster went down, to be followed shortly after by the brave. Thus they came to believe inevitable envelopment awaited a venturer to the middle of the lake.[11]

———————◆———————

Everybody Is Scared

———

Eluding deputy sheriffs and farmers, who have made many efforts to capture her, a wild woman, unknown and so strange in her behavior that people near St. Helens, OR, believe that she is an uncanny spirit, is wandering the hills near there, dressed only in a flowing gown and subsisting on berries and roots.

Who the woman is, where she came from, or what her age, no one knows. She made her appearance in the hills near St. Helens several days ago, and soon aroused the curiosity and later the fear of farmers in the vicinity by her peculiar actions in tearing down wire fences, wandering about at all hours of the night, frightening cattle, barnyard fowls and other animals that are unaccustomed to be disturbed at night.

From mild discussion and gossip of the woman's actions, there soon developed the fear that she was a ghost or a creature of the imagination. At first she was seen by only a few, but later, when watch was made, others distinctly saw the wraith hurrying through the brush at night, tearing down fences and wandering about near farmhouses at early hours in the morning. Farmers stayed up at night to capture the woman or discover who she was. She was frequently seen, but those who gave chase were unable to capture her.

Two days ago the sheriff's office was notified, and three deputies were sent out to capture the wild woman. The deputy sheriffs returned empty-handed, and reported that they were unable to find the woman.

So fleet of foot is the strange and mysterious creature that no one has been able to get close enough to her to describe her looks. Dressed only in a black robe, she flits about unmolested, because there is no one who has been able to put hands on her.

What puzzles the people of St. Helens is where the strange and demented woman came from. No report of missing insane people have been to the authorities, and they are unable to account for her appearance in the neighborhood. A resident of St. Helens, believing the woman might have escaped from Portland, reported the case to the police yesterday. The records were searched, but no report of a missing woman can be found on the register.[12]

---◆---

There is said to have been a wild man along the road between Camas Valley and Remote, who has been molesting the stage which carries mail on said route. Reports say one stage driver hired a boy to go with him and help protect the mail, for the sum of one dollar.[13]

---◆---

[1] *The San Francisco Call* (San Francisco, CA) January 20, 1900.

I found it interesting, given where he was living, that Hilstrom's "madness" took the form of a notion that the woods were full of "gorillas". Otherwise, this is just a tragic tale of a man with a gun shooting innocents which, sadly, reads like too many modern stories.

[2] *Daily Capital Journal* (Salem, OR) May 24, 1900.

[3] *Daily Capital Journal* (Salem, OR) May 25, 1900.

[4] *Statesman Journal* (Salem, OR) January 13, 1901.

This is the earliest mention I could find of the Coos County wild man, aka Kangaroo Man. It seems to have been an aggressive and ill-tempered bigfoot which roamed the region for years.

[5] *Daily Capital Journal* (Salem, OR) July 22, 1901.

[6] *The Medford Mail* (Medford, OR) December 13, 1901.

[7] *The Oregon Daily Journal* (Portland, OR) March 19, 1904.

[8] *Daily Capital Journal* (Salem, OR) March 25, 1904.

[9] *The Oregon Daily Journal* (Portland, OR) March 25, 1904.

[10] *Daily Capital Journal* (Salem, OR) March 30, 1904.

This report mirrors so many modern bigfoot encounters it is impossible for me to believe it is just coincidence. From the rock throwing and shaking of the cabins to trying the door - and perhaps especially the "revenge" aspect where the creature seems to have followed Mr. Ward to the Harrison cabin after he took a shot at the creature at his own cabin on a previous night. We have not only physical descriptions of the creatures which repeat over time but descriptions of the same behavior from over a century past through today.

[11] *East Oregonian* (Pendleton, OR) February 9, 1906.

Our interest lies with the "strange monster" of legend described herein. There are few details given but it is interesting that the brave met the creature in the solitude of the mountains. It's hard to say if it is anything more than a legend but, after all, many legends of the First Nations people which seem to describe bigfoot creatures describe, again, the same kinds of behaviors we see in these reports and hear from modern witnesses - so it is, in my view, worth noting the legend of Wallowa Lake.

[12] *Daily Capital Journal* (Salem, OR) July 30, 1906.

[13] *Roseburg Review* (Roseburg, OR) March 9, 1908.

IX. TERRORIZED BY A WILD MAN

OREGON 1911 - 1920

Woman Sees "Wild Man," Half Clothed, in Vicinity of Ardenwald

A report was received by Deputy Sheriff Phillips yesterday from a woman living near Ardenwald, that a man answering the description of the "wild man" seen in the woods near Ardenwald and the one who jumped on Gus Obrist last week, was seen again Monday afternoon. The woman said she saw him running along a fence through a patch of woods a little to the south of the woods into which Obrist's assailant fled and from which he emerged every morning at 2 or 3 o'clock.

This is the first time since the attack on Obrist that the man has been seen. The deputy sheriffs have been keeping their watch nightly at the farms around Ardenwald but have seen no sign of him.

The woman who says she saw the "wild man" Monday afternoon described him as being but partially clothed. She was much frightened but apparently he did not see her and ran through the woods, following the line of a wire fence.[1]

---◆---

"Wild Man" Scare Arises

HOOD RIVER, OR, Aug. 3 — Excitement prevailed in the west end residence section today when the news was scattered that there was a wild man in the

89

neighborhood, terrorizing woman and children. The stranger appeared to be insane and was hard to follow in his meanderings. Mr. Johnson took a shot at him but missed him.[2]

CONSTRUCTION CAMP WORKMEN IN TERROR

CLATSKANIE, OR, Oct. 10 — Telephonic information that a lunatic or drink crazed man is running amuck at Fishawk, a railroad construction camp a few miles southwest of here, was received shortly before noon today, and local police officials left immediately for the scene of the trouble.

Though particulars are meager because of the apparent nervousness of the man at the other end of the wire, given to understand that the belligerent, whose name was not given, had already killed four or five horses and that men in the camp were in mortal fear of him.

The camp is maintained by workmen employed on the Nehalem River Railroad company construction enterprise in Columbia County.[3]

DEER HUNTERS SEE WILD MAN

SIX FEET TALL, NAKED, LAUGHING LIKE A FIEND, BEARDED WILD MAN FRIGHTENS TOWN OF LELAND

LELAND, OR, Sept. 30 — Laughing like a maniac, walking like a man, six feet tall and as bare as Adam, Lower Crave Creek has a sensation in a wild creature that calls elusively for help, clambers over cliffs and fallen trees like an animal, and is stirring up the natives to fever heat.

Fire Warden Harry Schmidy, in company with Don Calvert and Roy Gearhart, spent the better part of a day trying to locate what appeared to be a man calling for help, supposed an unfortunate hunter, wounded or lost. But the search was fruitless, for as each time the spot was located from where the sounds came, nothing was there. The next day, Scotty Ray, while hunting, was attracted by a strange yellowish-looking creature scaling the cliffs across a canyon. Thinking it was a cougar, he got closer, and found it fully six feet tall, with beard, and all the appearances of a man walking upright, or on all fours at will. When it spied Scotty, this nature man let out such a continuous peal of demoniac laughter that Scotty lost his nerve and failed to shoot.

Maybe Joe Knowles is again growing a bunch of whiskers in the Oregon woods — who knows?[4]

————————◆————————

DESERT LAND TERRORIZED BY WILD MAN

———

A wild man on the Owyhee Desert is terrifying the cattle and sheep men of the territory lying along the Oregon and Nevada line. The authorities of Malheur County, OR have been asked to capture him. The disturber subsists on cattle and sheep which he kills, says *The Oregon Journal*.[5]

————————◆————————

[1] *The Oregon Daily Journal* (Portland, OR) June 21, 1911.

[2] *The Oregon Daily Journal* (Portland, OR) August 4, 1912.

[3] *The Oregon Daily Journal* (Portland, OR) October 10, 1913.

[4] *The Evening Herald* (Klamath Falls, OR) September 30, 1915.
It is reported that bigfoot creatures often mimic sounds of animals and people - and sometimes even things like machinery. Often I have read reports of the creatures making sounds like crying babies or women screaming. I have heard of other accounts where the creatures learn the names of peoples' pets. I believe this is done to lure people and/or their pets out into the woods. I think that the cries for help in this article were perhaps mimicry of the same sort. Also mentioned in this article is the bipedal-to-quadrupedal locomotion reported in so many bigfoot sightings.

[5] *The Times-Herald* (Burns, OR) March 13, 1920.

X. A MAN OF UNUSUALLY LARGE SIZE

WASHINGTON 1880 - 1897

A wild man has been discovered on the shores of Pend, Oreille Lake, Washington Territory.[1]

———————◆———————

A party from Gray's Harbor tells the Journal of the existence of a wild man in the woods near Aberdeen, whose appearance is so hideous as to strike with terror all who behold him.[2]

———————◆———————

A WILD MAN IN THE WOODS

OLYMPIA, July 13. — It is reported by parties who have recently arrived from Chambers Prairie that a crazy man has been seen in the woods near that place, and it is expected that a search will soon be instituted looking to a location of his abode. Two men who drove in to Olympia from that locality a few days ago, report having seen a nude man in the woods, near the road, acting in a very strange manner. They did not disturb him but drove on into the city. That night the same man was seen by a gentleman who was returning from the city, and was very much frightened at the peculiar antics of the nude man. The people of that neighborhood are becoming very much alarmed at these reports, and it is probable that they will soon turn out en masse and attempt to capture the object of their affright.[3]

———◆———

A wild man has been captured on an island near Nooksack. He has been terrorizing settlers for some time past. He wore only a breech cloth and carried an immense club. He cannot talk.[4]

———◆———

A wild man, who is said to be almost entirely nude, has been discovered roaming about the mountains west of Mayfield. His appearance strikes terror into the souls of residents of that vicinity.[5]

———◆———

A WILD MAN

———

A sure-enough wild man was seen in the Quillayute Mountains, near Cape Flattery, WA, a few days ago, and was closely and carefully scrutinized by Lawrence E. Doyle, a member of the Montana legislature, who is willing to furnish affidavits with his story. He says he was traveling through an unexplored timber belt when a man of unusually large size and splendid physique, hatless and with a heavy beard and shock of long hair, his arms and legs bare and his body partially clothed in skins, stepped out before him. Mr. Doyle was startled, and before he could say or do anything the wild man, after looking at him closely, walked quietly away. Mr. Doyle watched the man with his field glasses until he was out of sight, and is sure of the reality of his experience and of the wild man. Settlers in that region have claimed to have caught glimpses of a strange man dressed in skins, and a general hunt has been planned for the purpose of capturing him.[6]

———◆———

Deputy Sheriff Lane received a note yesterday from the Sand Point lighthouse keeper, stating that a wild man, who has been reported as running at large in that vicinity, had been seen. Mr. Lane will go out this morning to look into the matter.[7]

———◆———

[1] *Oakland Tribune* (Oakland, CA) September 21, 1880.

[2] *The Morning Astorian* (Astoria, OR) June 18, 1887.

[3] *The Seattle Post-Intelligencer* (Seattle, WA) July 14, 1888.

[4] *Washington Standard* (Olympia, WA) March 9, 1894.
While most likely a human the note about terrorizing settlers and carrying an immense club is of interest.

[5] *The Medford Mail* (Medford, OR) June 22, 1894.

[6] *The Morning Astorian* (Astoria, OR) March 21, 1896.

[7] *The Seattle Post-Intelligencer* (Seattle, WA) November 12, 1897.

XI. IT RUNS LIKE A GOBLIN

WASHINGTON 1905 - 1909

WILD MAN NEAR TACOMA

Lives Out of Doors and Flees From Human Beings

TACOMA, March 8. — The police are trying to capture a so-called "wild man," who has been roaming over the western suburbs for several weeks.

Capt. King believes the man is Adolf Metzger. King says Metzger shows a tendency to lapse into savagery and admits that for several weeks he has had the police endeavoring to capture Metzger.

Metzger appears to be sane, but he shows a tendency to live a solitary and even animal life. He has apparently forsworn anything savoring of human habitations, preferring to live in the open and foraging for a livelihood. Metzger is accustomed himself to do without clothing so far as the weather will permit. He runs at the approach of man. So far as known he has never offered violence to anyone, fleeing at the approach of a child the same as upon seeing a man. Those who have caught occasional glimpses of "the wild man" declare that he runs with incredible swiftness for a man and appears to be endowed with an almost animal-like power detecting the approach of people.

Several months ago Metzger was captured by the police and was kept on the chain gang for two weeks. Then he escaped, eluding persistent pursuit, and has not been seen since by the officers. He is thought to subsist on birds and small animals, which he traps, and from occasional forays on chicken coops of suburban residents.

Friends of Alfred White, of Puyallup, who, while waiting for an operation at a hospital here, mysteriously disappeared three weeks ago, made a search of the west end district today in hope that "the wild man" might be White. They found a lair in the thick brush near Franklin's school, in which a man has been sleeping, but could find no traces of the man.[1]

---◆---

LUNATIC RUNS AMOK

"A wild man is running loose in the woods out here, and the women and children are scared to death."

Such was the message Chief Deputy Sheriff Drew received over the telephone from Kerryston Friday morning. He at once dispatched Deputies McKinnon and Van Meer to gather in the lunatic, who had, it

was reported, just gone into a house adjoining A.S. Kerry's mill and upset a hot stove.[2]

---◆---

A wild man who lives in the brush and scares little girls is said to have been seen in the neighborhood of North Thirty-fourth and Stevens Streets, Tacoma, a number of times lately. The police are looking for him. They have tried several times and failed.[3]

---◆---

Tacoma has a wild man at large in her outskirts:

The dispatch does not say what he is wild about.[4]

---◆---

MONKEY HAUNTS
TACOMA TOWN

TACOMA, Oct. 12. — "Doc," a trained monkey belonging to Gentry Bro.s' circus, has caused the section of Tacoma in the neighborhood of Twenty-fourth and Twenty-third Streets and Pacific Avenue to be considered haunted for two weeks past.

Strange noises have been heard on roofs and balconies and

articles of different kinds have been disappearing from houses, and children and nervous women have seen a fantastical animal the size of which was described as being all the way from that of a big dog to that of a gorilla, flitting about the neighborhood.

It was simply "Doc" rustling a living and amusing himself. Eddie Mills arrived going back over the Gentry Bro.s route in hopes of locating the monkey. He heard of the haunted neighborhood and made a bee line for the locality. From what he knew of the monkey's habits he soon succeeded in locating him, but "Doc" at once declared a pronounced aversion to the "fish pots" of circus life, and Miles could not get near him. Tonight Mills is the most tired man in Tacoma. He declares he has climbed over the roofs from 40 to 50 houses, besides leaping fences and careening over hedgerows, and once in a while scaling a tree. "Doc" enjoyed the sport mightily, and at a late house was keeping a weather eye on Mills while looking for a place to spend the night.[5]

———————◆———————

Wild Man in Snohomish

———

SNOHOMISH, Dec. 7. — A wild man, strong and ferocious

as any beast that roams the wilds of the forests of the Northwest has created a reign of terror among the inhabitants of small towns along the Monte Cristo branch of the Northern Pacific, asserts a recent report. This animal, or man, whatever it is, has been seen several times during the past year in that part of the country. The latest person to see it is John O'Leary, a timber cruiser, who is now in Seattle.[6]

———————◆———————

WILD MAN ROAMS NORTHWEST WOODS

———

Creature More Beast Than Human Attacks Men in the Forest.

———

SEATTLE, Dec. 13. — A wild man, strong and ferocious as any beast that roams the northwestern forest, has created a reign of terror among the inhabitants of small Washington towns along the Monte Cristo branch of the Northern Pacific.

Nels Helgensen, recently from St. Paul, was attacked by the monster while in the brush, and says it walked upright and wore a few ragged garments about its abdomen and carried a rusty rifle, which was leveled at Helgensen, the hammers clicking several times without shooting. The strapping Swede grappled with his assailant and got the worst of the match.

Other loggers laughed at his story until the day before Thanksgiving when John O'Leary, a timber cruiser, went into the same neighborhood for game and had a similar experience. He went to sleep in a deserted cabin and was awaked by a demoniacal yell. Arising, he was knocked to the ground again, but hit the thing with an ax as it lunged for his throat. It then slunk off with a piteous half-human wail. In the moonlight O'Leary could see it move in an upright position. It had a hairy body and face.

Many old-timers at Granite Falls say they have seen the wild man, who is believed to be a Frenchman who took up a timber claim near Mount Pilchuk five years ago and disappeared mysteriously two years later. The supposition is that solitude drove him crazy, after which he lost much of his resemblance to the human by living wild.[7]

———————◆———————

WILD MAN CHASES PEOPLE IN WOODS

Terrorizes a Neighborhood Near Tacoma — Possibly an Escaped Lunatic.

TACOMA, WA, Feb. 5. — A wild man has thrown the residents of Oakland addition into a panic by his chasing 19-year-old Norma Byrd, while she was returning hime after visiting a neighbor.

Saturday morning, while on his way to work, a laboring man was attacked by the wild man, who tried to snatch the laborer's dinner pail. The laborer was passing a clump of bushes when the wild man stepped out and grabbed the pail. In surprise the laborer turned and jerked hard on the handle, spilling a portion of his lunch. At the same time he made a movement towards his hip pocket as if reaching for a gun. The wild man snatched a piece of bread from the ground and darted away through the brush.

Since Friday the wild man has been camping in a deserted shack in the woods near the schoolhouse. At times when seen by the children, he is said to be perfectly rational. At other times he dashes madly through the brush, or stands with his feet spread apart and beats his bare chest. He spent Sunday carrying pieces of bark and chips from various parts of the woods to the shack.

Thought to be Dangerous.

This morning Miss Byrd was passing along a path leading to the schoolhouse when the man suddenly jumped out of the bushes and took a few steps toward her. With a frightened cry, she ran toward the schoolhouse, where she reported her experience. The police were communicated with and several patrolmen were dispatched to search the woods.

About two weeks ago another wild man camped in the woods for several days, frightening women and children in the neighborhood. At times he would hop about like a frog or crawl about on his hands and knees. He suddenly disappeared.

The actions of the man now wandering about the woods lead the police to believe him to be Alex Lamore, who escaped from the asylum last week. Lamore is said to be a dangerous man. Asylum guards have had severe fights with him. It is feared that he will seriously injure or kill someone.[8]

A wild man in a nude state has been seen a number of times in the vicinity of South Tacoma and a general hunt of patrolmen and citizens is on for him. The man runs like a deer when sighted and succeeds in hiding in the brush.[9]

————————◆————————

WILD MAN RUNS LIKE GOBLIN

———

Early yesterday Dr. H.L. Smith notified the police that for the past 10 days a man has been seen in the neighborhood of Twentieth Ave. and Mill St. acting in a suspicious manner and seemingly demented. Yesterday a squad of police was put in search of the man, who again appeared, this time stark naked and raving mad. Men of the neighborhood, before the police arrived, tried to catch him, but he ran off like a deer to the south of the city.

He was last seen on Seventeenth, headed south, and is probably in eastern Oregon by this time, if he continued at the same rate of speed.[10]

————————◆————————

CHASED CRAZY MAN ALL DAY WITH BLOODHOUNDS

The Draper bloodhounds that are now owned by Detective Harry McDermott were used all day yesterday in an unsuccessful endeavor to run down the demented man who for several days has terrorized people south of the city by appearing suddenly before them stark naked and clawing the air. All Saturday and Sunday those connected with the sheriff;s office hunted the vicinity in that part of the city where the crazy man has appeared. The theory that the report was a hoax has been dissipated because too many people have told the officers that they saw the man.

At first he appeared dressed and only partially demented. Three days ago he appeared again, this time stark naked and raving mad. People who have seen him say that he can outrun a horse. As a last resort the hounds were sent for. Judging by the trail they followed the wild man certainly did some running and crossed and recrossed his own paths many times. A black soft hat, supposed to be his, has been found, but his other clothing is missing.[11]

WILD MAN CHASES WOMEN FOLKS

BELLINGHAM, May 9. — Running about wearing only a hat, a wild or insane man has selected West Geneva as his stamping ground and has badly frightened women by chasing them. Reports of the man's actions have been made to President Phillips of the Whatcom County Humane Society. The judge says he was told that the man chased one woman half a mile.[12]

WILD MAN MUST BE PUBLIC BRAINSTORM

Is this wild man business a hoax? Officers are beginning to believe it is, for every time one of them responds to a call the wild man has just disappeared again. As a general thing the person who informs the police always hangs up the telephone immediately afterward without giving his name.

Last night there was another call, this time from the vicinity of Spokane College. When Jake Warner reached the scene, as usual, the crazy one had just moved. At diverse times he appears naked, or dressed, the police think according to the mood of the person who "sees" him.

This wild man business has been going on now for a month, without an officer seeing him, but many people claiming to have better luck. Judging by the stories, the man climbs trees like a monkey, runs like a deer and wears a beard like a patriarch or pirate.[13]

———————◆———————

WILD MAN MAKES ATTACK ON WOMAN

———

Steilacoom is all excitement about a "wild man" who attacked three women Tuesday night, chasing them from the woods with frightful cries. A posse of men searched the woods Tuesday night but was unable to locate him. The women say that he looks hideous and is scantily clad. A 16-year-old girl was the first to be attacked by the man. While passing along the road he rushed out upon her but she was too swift for him and ran screaming into town. After her, two married women had similar experiences.

It was thought that the man was insane and had escaped from the asylum, but it is reported that no one is missing from there.[14]

———————◆———————

[1] *The Evening Statesman* (Walla Walla, WA) March 8, 1905.

[2] *The Seattle Star* (Seattle, WA) June 9, 1905.

[3] *The Spokane Press* (Spokane, WA) February 28, 1906.

[4] *The Wenatchee Daily World* (Wenatchee, WA) September 26, 1907.

[5] *The Spokane Press* (Spokane, WA) October 12, 1907.
As the "escaped gorilla" is the solution given so often by newspaper reporters I thought I would include an example of an actual escaped monkey. While we are not sure exactly what kind of primate "Doc" was, he was valuable enough for the circus to know he was missing and to send someone after him. Gorillas, being that much bigger and much more valuable would certainly be missed, and hunted for by the circus managers - yet in most of the bigfoot reports claimed to be "escaped gorillas" by newspapers at the time there is no note of a specific circus from which the gorilla escaped, much less of people trying to recapture the animal.

[6] *The Evening Statesman* (Walla Walla, WA) December 7, 1907.

[7] *The Oregon Daily Journal* (Portland, OR) December 13, 1907.

[8] *The Oregon Daily Journal* (Portland, OR) February 5, 1908.

[9] *The Evening Statesman* (Walla Walla, WA) April 16, 1908.

[10] *The Spokane Press* (Spokane, WA) May 2, 1908.

[11] *The Spokane Press* (Spokane, WA) May 4, 1908.

[12] *The Seattle Star* (Seattle, WA) May 9, 1908.

[13] *The Spokane Press* (Spokane, WA) May 26, 1908.
We get more information on the Spokane wild man of 1908 who, at times, seems to be a human - but then we read these little details like bloodhounds not being able to find him; running as fast as a deer or a horse; climbing trees like a monkey; and so on - which seem to point to something other than human.

[14] *The Tacoma Times* (Tacoma, WA) July 15, 1909.

XII. ATTACKED BY A MYSTERIOUS MONSTER

WASHINGTON 1913 - 1921

A posse up in Washington is hunting a wild man — probably some Democrat who failed to get a job from the Wilson administration. That's why he is so wild.[1]

————◆————

'BOSCO' LEAPS OUT OF BRUSH ON WORKMAN

Laborer Attacked by Mysterious Monster on Monlake Blvd., Near Boathouse.

HURLS GREAT WEIGHT

Hits His Victim in Back With Iron Missile Wrapped Up in Paper.

Women and children in the University district are terrorized today by the presence of a wild man in that vicinity.

The police are searching the brush for him, following his attack on P. Delphente, a laborer, 1648 Lane St, early today.

Delphente is employed by the Independent Asphalt Company on Montlake Boulevard, near the University boathouse.

He arrived on the job early this morning and walked into the bushes to pick some berries, when he was set upon by the wild man.

After a struggle, during which "Bosco" attempted to strike Delphante with an object wrapped in paper, the workman escaped and ran, only to receive a blow from the object in the back, causing a painful bruise.

The object proved to be a window weight, weighing about 25 pounds.

"Bosco" is described as the regulation wild man, with long matted hair and whiskers; teeth resembling long yellow tusks; hands like eagle talons; hairy chest; eyes like Svengali's, only moreso, and wearing only enough clothes to get past the board of censors.

Residents think it is the same wild man who caused a reign of terror in that neighborhood last winter.[2]

––––––––––◆––––––––––

BUGHOUSE BOSCO, VARSITY WILD MAN, MAKES LUNCHES OFF DOGS; BITES OFF TREES

––––––

Bughouse Bosco, the bushman, the terror of the University district, is still at large today, despite a determined search by the police yesterday.

Bosco is the man who leaped upon an Italian workman on the Montlake Boulevard, within a hundred yards of the University canoe house on Lake Washington yesterday morning. Not content with choking his victim with his claws, he threw a heavy piece of iron at him and nearly caved in the workman's ribs.

After that he fled into the brush again.

The Italian described him as a wild eyed giant, clad much like Robinson Crusoe before he learned the art of tailoring. He says Bosco has long, matted hair, forming a thatch on his head; his evil face is almost hidden by a tangled growth of black beard, through which long, yellow tusks protrude.

The workman would not go near the spot yesterday afternoon. But he stood across the roadway and pointed. When it became necessary to designate exact spots, he threw stones, but he would not approach the thicket from whence the wild man had sprung on him.

• • •

Just at the edge of the thicket is a little plot of sand, and here the marks of bare feet were plainly visible. It was at this point that the scuffle occurred.

The foreman for the Independent Asphalt Co., who declined to give his name, said that during his examination of the thicket shortly after the assault, he found several alder trees, averaging six inches in diameter, lying across the path, with evidence that they had been bitten down by Bosco to delay pursuers.

Motorcycle Patrolman J.A. Thomas, with a member of the mounted squad, found evidence that Bosco had employed a large log to kill what appeared to have been a yellow dog, near the lake shore, about 200 yards south of the boathouse.

Yellow hair lay here and there, and a few crunched bones, but no flesh.

Thomas believes the wild man ate the dog.

The log, measuring two feet in diameter, was broken in the middle.

• • •

Evidence that a dog was following him was brought out in an interview with Mrs. Jack Ehritin, who lives near the boathouse, and who was the only one who witnessed the encounter.

A few minutes after the Italian had been attacked, she declares she saw a form slink out to the water's edge and then dart back again. A yellow dog, with dirty hair, followed.

Mrs. Ehrlin was walking along the railroad track with a pail of water when the wild man attacked his victim. She saw him dig his talons into the man's throat, saw the Italian fight for breath, and heard him finally shriek for help. The wild man then fled.

• • •

Last night when Frank Swaps, fireman at the University power house, which is just across the N.P. tracks from the thicket, went down to adjust the electric pump near the boat house, he was startled by a weird, unearthly cry, which seemed to come from the lake grass in the swamp at the head of the bay.

Swaps doesn't believe in ghosts, and after a moment he shrugged his shoulders and went inside.

But when he came out in a few moments he was just in time to see the wild man trot noiselessly down the railroad bank from the direction of the swamp and plunge into the lake, not 50 feet from where he stood in the shadows.

Swaps waited patiently, and soon Bosco emerged and squatted on the bank.

He seemed to be nibbling. Creeping closer to investigate, Swaps encountered a twig, which snapped. The wild man fled. Swaps found a half-eaten fish.

• • •

Night before last the wild man peered into the engine room door of the power house about 10:30. Engineer William Auckland attempted to coax him inside, but he became suspicious and went away. Auckland chased him to the tracks, but lost him in the darkness.

Bursar Herbert T. Condon of the University has been greatly puzzled the past few days by the discovery of huge footprints in the asphalt walks of the campus, impressed there before the asphalt hardened from the heat of the day. Last night he declared he believed them the footprints of Bosco.[3]

BOSCO IS ON JOB AGAIN

Bosco, the wild man of the U. of W. campus, is on the job again, according to reports turned in to the police by two women of the University district, who claim they were chased by a man dressed like "September Morn" on the campus last night. One of the women, whose names the police refuse to make public, fell and was injured during the chase.[4]

BOSCO, BUSHMAN, IS OUT AGAIN

"Bosco the Bushman," who terrorized the residents in the University district a month ago, is again at work. This time he is near Medina. T.W. Flynn telephoned Under Sheriff McCormick today that the wild man was yelling in a dense thicket and apparently seeking the blood of all who dared pass the spot.

Citizens fear to tackle Bosco. He has a habit of biting trees in two. He ate a dog and hurled a heavy boulder at an Italian laborer recently.

Deputy Sheriffs Sullivan and Smith, fully armed, started

for Medina at noon and will try to subdue and capture Bosco.[5]

———————◆———————

RUNNING WILD MAN NEWEST CAMPUS DOPE

With opening day of the winter term at the University approaching, faculty and regents are making every effort to capture or chase away the mysterious wild man, who, for nearly a year now, has been terrifying women students by attacking them on lonely parts of the campus.

Not only did he appear at numerous times throughout last winter, but he has lurked around the campus all summer, and only a week ago he nearly frightened the life out of a young woman on the university grounds.

Every strategy that could be thought of has been employed to capture him. Both faculty and male students under the direction of Bursar Herbert T. Condon, have patrolled the campus hours at a time night after night. But the man sneaks away when men are around.

He is bold, though, in the presence of women, attacking groups of two and even three when he finds them alone and unguarded.

Indignant male students will make it one of their season's activities this year to capture the wild man, just as Dobie's men make it a point to corral the football championship.

And if they DO capture him, tragedy threatens to be writ in the annals of the institution.[6]

———————◆———————

OR MAYBE BOSCO

Sheriff Hodge and Deputies Elliott and Bush beat about the woods in the vicinity of O'Brien Sunday without being able to locate a "wild man" who had been reported in that section.

The sheriff believes the man may be Fred Trotto, who recently escaped from the Medical Lake Asylum.[7]

———————◆———————

'BOSCO' SCARES CAMPUS CO-EDS

"Wild Man" Appears Again; Girls Don't Go Out Alone.

HE HAS ATTACKED 'EM

The wild man has appeared again at the university campus.

Whether is is the same man who last year terrorized the

women of the student body, or a new recruit, he is emphatically there, and as a result of his attempting to attack several girls on the campus at night, Dean of Women Coldwell has advised all university women not to appear on campus or secluded streets after 5 pm except in groups of three or more.

The "wild man" made his presence felt to such an extent last year that a student patrol was organized in an attempt to capture him, but he attacked only when he was sure no help was near. The students refer to him as "Bosco."

In spring two suspects were captured and lodged in jail.

The "wild man" has been haunting the campus for a number of years. Two years ago several members of the S.A.E. fraternity captured a fellow. After an indignant group of girls at the dormitory had positively identified him as the man who had pursued them, the boys washed off his mud and war paint and taught them not to go too strong on circumstantial evidence.

He was one of the fraternity men, "made up" for the occasion.[8]

———————◆———————

SHERIFF'S BLOODHOUNDS HUNT FOR WILD MAN

Prairie Region People Terrorized By Antics of Strange Individual — Keeps on the Jump

Answering a call from several citizens of Spanaway, Sheriff Longmire, accompanied by deputies Stenseo and Frank Longmire, left early today with the bloodhound Torger in search for a wild man reported to have been terrorizing the countryside for two weeks.

The mysterious man is said to be a short, dark complexioned person.

He runs like a deer and lives in the woods.

He has been seen on several occasions at Roy, McKenna, Spanaway and other prairie towns.

Keeps on Move.

He has frightened several young girls and women, and the communities are so stirred up that many persons are living in continual fear.

A large delegation of farmers aided in the hunt.

The wild man will appear suddenly in the open, and after

making insane motions, he will dart off into the woods and disappear, say those who have seen him.

He never appears twice in the same place.

One night he will be reported at Spanaway and the next thing he will bob up at Yelm.

He is described as being a short man with a very black mustache. He wears a black suit and occasionally goes without a hat. Men living in the district have been unable to get within hailing distance as he immediately turns and runs.

Children See Him.

Children living near the Vogel ranch about one and three-quarters miles northeast of Spanaway say they saw the man looking around a tree at them last night as they were getting water from a well. They screamed, and he disappeared into the darkness.

A posse of 20 farmers scoured the woods, but could find no traces.

Sheriff Longmire and Torger looked into every vacant house in the district today.

County Speed Officer Chilberg will be stationed near Spanaway the next few days, patrolling the wooded districts.[9]

————◆————

CO-EDS SCARED BY "WILD MAN" AT UNIVERSITY

———

A sub-rosa man hunt is in progress on the university campus to capture an elusive wild man whose after dark pastime has been to terrorize co-eds.

He made a sudden appearance Thursday night, stepping from the shadows and letting out a yell, when Miss Gertrude Elliott, in charge of the campus commons, and two girl students were passing the home economics building.

They could not see his face, but they noticed he was only partly dressed.

Because students and authorities of the university have been trying to catch the fellow for more than a year, the three young women planned to summon aid.

Miss Elliott Shows Courage

When Miss Elliott and one of her friends stepped behind two trees, the third girl ran for Night Officer Bloom, who patrols the campus.

But the so-called wild man suddenly turned and ran before the posse of Officer Bloom and his three feminine assistants could get a start.

The story of the wild man seen Thursday night, however, is only the latest of a long series of alarming appearances of the strange-acting man, or men, as the case may be.

He's Been Known Four Years

For four years there have been intermittent campaigns to catch him. Every few weeks some girl, or group of girls, has been frightened.

A year ago all the men of the university were called together at an assembly, where the situation was discussed by Dean Priest and Comptroller Condon.

The men students were told what was going on, and asked to suggest some way of capturing the wild man.

No practical method was evolved.

No Girls Alone After Dark

The women held assemblies. Rules were passed that no co-ed should go on the campus alone after dark. There were weeks when the fellow would not be seen. Then he would bob up again, appearing suddenly from the thick underbrush lining the campus walks. Finally much of the brush was cut out.

One night in February, 1916, he followed a young woman from one of the streets outside the campus over the path that leads to the girls dormitory.

Girl Hits Him

She permitted him to get close to her, suddenly turned and struck him in the face with her suitcase. Then she ran into the dormitory.

At other times he has hidden in the brush and peeped out when the girls passed by. Often he lets out a yell, and then goes scurrying away into the dark.

Golfer Hunts Him

C.J. Horton, professional golfer of the University Golf Club, was made a special officer recently, and is on the lookout for the "wild" man.

Brief descriptions in the hands of the authorities at the university indicate that the fellow is thin and tall. He often wears a cap, and is believed to be comparatively young.

Some think he is the same man who has been seen near the Green Lake School and at some of the playgrounds.[10]

———————◆———————

A wild man is terrorizing people in the vicinity of the village of Humptulips, Washington, and one wonders if he didn't go wild trying to fathom the origin of such a name for a town.[11]

———————◆———————

Report Wild Woman in Riverton woods

An insane woman, running wildly through the woods near the sanitarium at Riverton, was reported Monday morning to be alarming residents of the Riverton district. According to the report she has been living several days on blackberries and runs away frightened when approached by the residents. Deputies were sent out Monday morning to search the woods.[12]

———————◆———————

[1] *The Los Angeles Times* (Los Angeles, CA) April 20, 1913.

[2] *The Seattle Star* (Seattle, WA) July 2, 1914.
So begins the "Bosco" wild man saga which, as you will read, continues for some time. Bosco sounds like a bigfoot to me - besides the description of his appearance what human could so easily throw a 25 pound weight?

[3] *The Seattle Star* (Seattle, WA) July 3, 1914.
"Bosco" continues with the oft-noted bigfoot behaviors of window-peeking; dog killing/eating; trees broken down across paths; and huge bare footprints left in his wake.

[4] *The Seattle Star* (Seattle, WA) July 20, 1914.

[5] *The Seattle Star* (Seattle, WA) August 1, 1914.

[6] *The Seattle Star* (Seattle, WA) August 29, 1914.

[7] *The Seattle Star* (Seattle, WA) June 21, 1915.

[8] *The Seattle Star* (Seattle, WA) October 5, 1915.

[9] *The Tacoma Times* (Tacoma, WA) February 26, 1916.
While this article mentions suits and hats on the wild man, it also states that no one could get very close to him; that he ran like a deer; covered great distances in short times; was seen tree-peeking as bigfoot often are; and that he was terrifying the community. Perhaps those suits and hats were body hair and a sagittal crest (the feature which, it is presumed, sometimes gives bigfoot a "pointy" or coned head, as reported by many witnesses).
The stories of these various wild men - in this and many other articles in this volume - "terrifying" people are somewhat puzzling. The West was still a fairly "wild" place at this time - peopled by farmers and loggers and railroad men. Aside from the First Nations people who had lived there for centuries before, these residents were people who had either made the hard journey from the eastern states, or were not many generations removed from those who had. It seems to me it would take something a bit more intimidating than a short man in a dark suit to "terrify" these people. They must have had to deal with much worse on many occasions (bears, cougar, wolves, etc).

[10] *The Seattle Star* (Seattle, WA) November 25, 1916.
The last of the "Bosco" articles I could find, though he is not named as such in this account. Still, someone or something which couldn't be caught prowled the University of Washington campus for years.

[11] *Morning Register* (Eugene, OR) July 27, 1919.

[12] *The Seattle Star* (Seattle, WA) July 25, 1921.

INDEX OF PLACE NAMES

Q

Quillayute Mountains 95

R

Redding 46
Remote 86
Riverton 113
Roseburg 82
Rubio Canyon 37
Rumsey 26-27, 29

S

San Bernardino 35, 46, 53, 61
San Bernardino County 46
San Bernardino Mountains 60
San Diego 16
San Diego County 14
San Dimas Canyon 48
San Emigdio 36
San Francisquito Canyon 62
San Gabriel Valley 48
San Joaquin 8
San Joaquin County 2
San Jose 13
San Mateo County 59
Sand Point 95
Santa Cruz 17
Santa Monica 51
Santa Rosa 34
Sears Point 49
Seattle 99
Sierra Mountains 5, 7
Silver Canyon 18
Sixes 83
Sixes River 81
Snow Mountain 23
Snohomish 99
South Umpqua River 70
Spanaway 110-111
Spokane College 102
Spreckels Quarry 49

Squaw Valley 5
Steilacoom 103
St Helens 85-86
Stanford University 51
Stanislaus County 3
Stillwater 13
Stockton 62
Sur 44

T

Tacoma 97-101
Toulumne County 2
Tulare County 5
Tule River 12

U

University of Washington
105-112

V

Vale 76
Vining Creek Canyon 22
Visitacion Hills 59

W

Wallowa Lake 84
Wallowa Valley 84
Washington Corners 3
West Geneva 102
Whatcom County 102
Woodland 26, 32

Y

Yelm 111
Yolo 9
Yolo County 28
Yreka 59, 63
Yuba Mountains 47

ABOUT THE AUTHOR

Timothy Renner is an illustrator, author, and folk musician living in Pennsylvania. His illustrations have appeared in the pages of various books, magazines, fanzines and comics as well as on many record and CD covers. Since 1995, Timothy has been making music both solo and with his band, Stone Breath. Stone Breath has released over a dozen albums. Timothy is the creator of "Strange Familiars", a podcast concerning the paranormal, weird history, folklore and the occult. He makes regular appearances on the paranormal radio show, "Where Did the Road Go?", and has appeared as a guest on many other podcasts and radio programs, including "Coast to Coast AM".

Contact Timothy via email: TimeMothEye@gmail.com

www.StrangeFamiliars.com

Other books by Timothy:
Beyond the Seventh Gate, 2016
Bigfoot in Pennsylvania, 2017

Author photo by A.E. Hoskin.

BIGFOOT IN PENNSYLVANIA:
A HISTORY OF WILD MEN,
GORILLAS, AND OTHER HAIRY MONSTERS
IN THE KEYSTONE STATE

Made in the USA
Middletown, DE
09 September 2023

38018606R00076